THE
HOWL
OF THE
WHISPER

What People Are Saying About
The Howl of The Whisper

"This is not another 'self-help' book. This is a guide to finding your authentic self and using your inherent strengths to forge a powerful future."

David Cook, CEO
Learning Ecosystems Design LLC

"This book reads like a conversation with a dear friend. MaryAnn takes you through her personal journey to authenticity in a way that is relatable and eminently relevant. This book will become a must read for my own clients as they learn their strengths and make proactive decisions to improve their lives!"

Carla Nye, DNP, CPNP-PC, CNE, CHSE, Nursing Professor,
Healthcare Leadership Consultant,
Gallup® Certified Strengths Coach

"This book is a refreshing, insightful, and incredibly accessible guide to discovering your true strengths and unlocking the power of your authentic voice. Written in everyday language that's easy to understand and impossible to put down, it feels like a conversation with a wise friend who truly gets you. Whether you're just starting out on your personal growth journey or looking to reconnect with your inner purpose, this book offers practical tools, relatable stories, and an empowering message that stays with you long after the last page. An absolute must-read for anyone ready to show up as their real self and thrive because of it. It's also a great resource for businesses—large and small—seeking to cultivate authenticity, engagement, and true leadership within their teams."

Jeffrey W. Crowe, TMP
Director; Kentucky Experiences
Heaven Hill Distillery

"*The Howl of the Whisper* is a powerful, heart-opening journey into the voice that holds so many of us back—our inner critic. If you've ever wrestled with self-doubt, shame, or the weight of your past, this book offers more than hope—it offers a way through. "With striking vulnerability, the author brings her own inner critic into the light, not just to share her story, but to show you how to rewrite your own. Her honesty is disarming, her storytelling deeply relatable, and her insights boldly life-changing.

This is the kind of book that doesn't just inspire—it stays with you. It calls you forward, invites you to take up space, and reminds you that you are so much more than the voice that tells you to play small."

Sara E. Harvey
Founder & CEO, innertelligence Coaching
Chopra Center® Certified Meditation &
Mind-Body Health Instructor
Gallup® Advanced Certified Strengths Coach

THE
HOWL
OF THE
WHISPER

Calm Your Inner Critic,
Discover Your Strengths, and
Give Voice to the Authentic You

MARYANN GRAMIG

Publishing support provided by
Ignite Press
55 Shaw Ave. Suite 204
Clovis, CA 93612
www.IgnitePress.us

ISBN: 979-8-9930146-0-9
ISBN: 979-8-9930146-1-6 (Hardcover)
ISBN: 979-8-9930146-2-3 (E-book)

For bulk purchases and for booking, contact:

MaryAnn Gramig
hello@calmyourinnercritic.com
https://www.calmyourinnercritic.com

Trigger warning: Contains sensitive content and mentions of abuse, mental health, eating disorders, and other topics that may be distressing.

Library of Congress Control Number: 2025917821

Cover design by Usman Tariq
Edited by Zoe Herold
Interior design by Jetlaunch

FIRST EDITION

For Kyle, John Paul, and Annemarie—

You've inspired me from your very first day.
I am humbled to have been chosen to be your mother.

Table of Contents

Foreword

It is an honor and a privilege to write this foreword for a book authored by someone who has been both a trusted friend and an unwavering guide in my professional and personal journey. Over the years, she has worn many hats in my life—career coach, mentor, and at times, a therapist of sorts. She has an extraordinary ability to see beyond the surface, helping me uncover my greatest strengths and realize potential I often overlooked. When leadership challenges arose or opportunities seemed daunting, she became my "go-to" resource, coaching me through with wisdom, compassion, and the very same exercises you will find within these pages.

Her story, woven throughout this book, is as raw as it is inspiring. It invites us to confront one of life's toughest adversaries—the inner critic. That voice, so often disguised as logic or caution, can hold us back from the success and fulfillment we deserve. This book challenges us to meet that critic head-on with honesty and courage, because real transformation only happens when we dare to do the deep, authentic work.

One of her most powerful reminders appears within these chapters: *"Your authentic voice is your greatest, most powerful tool for calming your inner critic. Why? Because Authentic You came first."* Those words resonate deeply because they speak to a truth many of us forget—that before doubt, before fear, before the noise of the world, there was our truest self. Reclaiming that self is not a passive process. It demands perseverance, reflection, and a commitment to showing up as we are—fully and unapologetically.

I speak from experience when I say that these lessons are not theoretical—they are transformative. I have had the privilege of serving in two major leadership capacities. For 10 years, I served as President and CEO of Shelby County, KY Tourism, where I led major public relations, marketing, and advocacy efforts that grew tourism revenues by an incredible 1,800%. Today, I serve as Executive Vice President of the Kentucky Derby Museum, where I have co-led the organization for over five years, driving an impressive 38% increase in gross revenues. These roles have been deeply rewarding, but they have also required continuous self-awareness and growth. The principles in this book mirror the very work I've relied on to navigate challenges, lead with authenticity, and foster meaningful impact.

And that is why I believe this book is for everyone. Whether you are a college student preparing to launch your career, a young professional striving to establish yourself, a seasoned leader managing complex responsibilities, or someone approaching retirement and reflecting on your legacy—there is something here for you. We all have strengths to embrace, blind spots to confront, and inner critics to quiet. This book provides a fresh, practical approach to becoming self-aware so that you can lead your life—not just your career—with clarity and authenticity.

This is not simply a guide; it is a companion for anyone ready to silence "Patsy," as the author aptly named her own inner critic, and embrace the life that awaits when authenticity takes the lead. If you approach these pages with openness and honesty, the work you do here has the power to change not only how you lead but also how you live.

I am grateful to call the author a friend, a coach, and a source of enduring wisdom. It is my hope that her words will inspire you as profoundly as they have inspired me.

—Katie Fussenegger, CTA, CTIS, TMP
Executive Vice President, Kentucky Derby Museum

Introduction

There's a voice that resides deep within each of us. It's the voice of our true, authentic self that urges us to think, play, act, create, do, and just *be* all we're designed to be with joyful abandon. Some hear it early and clearly and follow it unashamedly all their life.

For the rest of us, the way we were created, the way that feels closest to our own heart, soul, mind, and body became "not good enough" somewhere along the way. Our authentic self was "wrong" somehow, and we felt like everyone else already knew it.

Can you relate? If I had to guess, I'd say you picked up this book because of your story of living life on other people's terms by rules and conditions you didn't set up to satisfy someone else's agenda. Little by little, your inner critic took control of your life, and you've long ignored the whisperings of your soul—your authentic self, yearning to howl in a fearless, joyful, unstifled, glorious voice.

Maybe you feel the stirrings of your soul rising, and that persistent whisper is growing... Well, *bravo* to you. It's no accident you're reading this book. You're at the precipice of discovering, embracing, and elevating your genuine voice from a faint whisper to a heroic howl. You're recognizing your authentic voice and honoring it by paying attention, and it brought you here. Others may be searching for your whisper, or you could be at the precipice of unleashing your howl.

No matter where you are on your journey, you're on the right path, my courageous friend, because you're stepping out. You're exactly where you need to be. Not too early. Not too late. Most definitely, not too late. I worried about that, too. Had I wasted too much time? Had I missed my chance? Well, no. And no.

But I've been where you may be now. In my late 40s, I had no hobbies and was strained under a mountain of pain and self-loathing. After devoting myself to being a mother and military wife for decades, building my nonprofit career in the background, I felt called to do more with my life and had no idea where to start. My future seemed foggy and just out of reach. Until I found what was missing, and it was there all along.

By simply being intentional about using my strengths, my life transformed. I went from a compliant army wife to a fierce momma bear and from a behind-the-scenes nonprofit executive to a face of the brand business owner. And I returned to my childhood pursuit of acting. These shifts invited my authentic self to emerge and, in turn, empowered me to begin calming my inner critic.

I'm still on the journey, but my transformation was so profound, I eventually left the 9-to-5 job model, became a certified Gallup® Strengths Coach, and opened AuthenticA®, a coaching & consulting firm. I later earned my Advanced Strengths Coaching certification. Today, I speak, coach, consult, and write to empower others to derive joy and confidence from the same strengths-based approach that redefined my life. To see my clients (you'll meet some of them in this book) find their missing ingredient and infuse it into their lives energizes me every day.

The Missing Ingredient—Authentic You

On my self-improvement journey, I read LOTS of self-help books. Maybe you have, too. At any given time, my nightstand would be stacked with at least a dozen books, leaning like the tower of Pisa that I prayed would give me the answers I so desperately sought. I often doubted if I was even asking the right questions. After disappointing outcome after disappointing outcome, I realized I must be using the self-help books all wrong. I tried to follow them exactly according to the prescribed steps spelled out on the pages, but they never worked for me. Something was wrong with... me, I surmised.

With the help of my CliftonStrengths® report, I realized there were two flaws in my approach. Firstly, I was trying to extract answers from every book I read that would be specific to *my* "why" questions. Secondly, the remedies offered felt misaligned, inauthentic. But why wouldn't they? They all had one thing in common. They left out the most important part of the equation. *Me*. I was trying to mold myself into someone else's cookie-cutter solution or method.

When you believe that you don't have control over your choices and doubt that what you want counts as legitimate success, you're constantly looking outward for direction. I felt like I was following the GPS coordinates to someone else's house, hoping I'd reach my home. It didn't work. I always ended up with the band-aids falling off my wounds and feeling lost, confused, and that I failed—again.

Don't get me wrong. I'm not saying we can't learn from others. We're meant to do that, and I hope you'll learn from the mistakes I write about in this book. But there's a very important distinction you must remember: No one is more qualified on the subject of you than *you*. Combine that with a coach or mentor who can empower you through your natural strengths, and you'll arrive at your destination: calm, confidence, and success—the joy and peace of being at home in your own skin.

Oh, you can fake it by borrowing from someone else's success story, but that will always feel artificial. You know what happened every time I tried to mimic a guru's success plan? It was a façade. The rocks were loose under my feet. After a while, I'd lose my footing and slide back down the mountain. Sound familiar? Yours could be crumbling now. You're losing your footing. Those sharp rocks are painful, and not being yourself is exhausting.

So, maybe, just maybe, you've gone about self-development all wrong before, as I did. Until I found the missing ingredient, my authentic God-given self, "Authentic You," as I like to call it.

Before you read any further, I must warn you... Trading being held hostage to the tyranny of your inner critic for living a life of fearless authenticity is only for those truly ready, those who have really had enough of the status quo, and are committed to ending patterns of behavior that repeat in an ongoing, suffocating cycle. For readers brave enough to move forward, this path leads away from figuring out what's "wrong" with you, ignoring your intuition's whispers in favor of what's popular, and trying to be someone you're not. This trajectory leads to building the fortitude to silence the inner critic, living a purpose-filled life of self-leadership, and unleashing the joyful howl of Authentic You.

What This Book Is About

I share a lot of personal stories, like the origins of my inner critic that helped me survive foster care, being molested, and anorexia, and how I grew to be a judgmental, perfectionist Army wife, afraid to be revealed as a fraud. I take you through losing my voice as a child and finally hearing it again when my teenage daughter was critically ill. As you read about my life, notice what's similar or different in your experiences, how they might've shaped you, and what strategies may work best for you.

The notions of an inner voice with a "whisper" and a "howl" are metaphorical and invite you to interpret their meaning for yourself. This book has many metaphors and comparisons, so you can fill in your blanks. Rather than trying to address every possible variable of how the inner critic pops up in daily life, I provide rich illustrations onto which you can write your truth. For example, in Chapter 4, I compare the battle with the inner critic to a war. Each reader may relate the wartime metaphors to their own parallel experiences, which may differ widely.

The art of this book is balanced by the specifics of its solutions. To make a genuine resolution and begin anew, I'll show you how to use everything that's right about you to stand up to the bully inside your head. You can design the rest of your life based upon trusting in how the One who designed you with all of the amazing talents, strengths, and courage you possess. Fortunately, instead of guessing what your unique qualities are, you can take the Gallup® CliftonStrengths® Assessment, like I did, and make progress as fast as clicking your heels and repeating, "There's no place like home." Learning your strengths is like coming home to yourself. I was homesick in ways I didn't even realize.

At the end of each chapter, you'll be reminded to visit the back of the book to the guided exercise section called *Pause and Practice.* There, you'll have the gift of space to consider what you're discovering about your true self, reflect on where you've been, and take small and meaningful steps forward. Each chapter's exercises provide you with the insights and action steps necessary to identify the path that best suits you. I invite you to come along with me and lay the foundation, so you'll recognize your strengths, not just to survive but to thrive again and again.

Although taking the Gallup® CliftonStrengths® Assessment isn't required to benefit from this book, I'm including the website address for it. Everyone should know their natural strengths. And you especially should because in this book I'm going to teach you how to put them to work for you and your goals and dreams. It's a low-cost, simple assessment that takes no more than thirty minutes to complete. Your results will be delivered to your email, with resources to help you discover Authentic You. I don't gain from your purchase, but you will.

Select the CliftonStrengths Top 5 Assessment at https://store. gallup.com

Now, grab a pen, a highlighter, or both. This book's meant to be underlined, notes written in the margins, and dog-eared. This isn't a book you loan to a friend. This is your book. Send them a copy and a highlighter with the same admonition I'm giving you to *use* it.

Choosing What Fits You

I *love* my red rain boots. I wear them often on walks in the woods. I especially love tromping in the creek. Creek tromping takes me back to my childhood when summers meant being barefoot from morning 'til night, playing in small streams, catching salamanders, and playing tricks on my annoying younger brother. I felt free and connected to the One Creator Divine. I knew I was an integral part of it all somehow. I felt connected to Mother Earth. I don't tromp around barefoot in creeks much anymore since that unfortunate parasite incident. (And, no, that story won't be coming soon to bookstores near you. Trust me, you wouldn't want to read it.)

I could choose any other kind of footwear for my woodland mini-adventures. I have sneakers, walking shoes, hiking boots, paddock boots, and there's an old pair of Army boots lying around somewhere from my college ROTC days; I'm sure they're dry rotted by now. Any of these would provide me the support I need to walk a stony creek path. But they're no fun. They're boring. And I feel dull in them.

The sneakers and walking shoes remind me I should be exercising more. Yuck. Who needs that guilt? The hiking boots remind me of my best friend, Carla, explaining that hiking boots are for *hiking*, as in steep inclines, and not what I like to refer to as "wa-hiking." Or, as she says, "just plain walking." Whatever. The paddock boots remind me of being thrown during an English saddle lesson. And my Army boots, well, as I said, dry-rotted, like the goal of serving in the military that illness derailed. But my red rain boots? Perfection. I feel like *me* when I'm in them. I take risks, jump gullies, and test the strength of dead fall branches. I'm more confident in testing out my footing on an uncertain rock in the creek bed. I simply feel like, well, *me*.

A psychologist once told me that we're most free to express ourselves up to age six. Unashamedly engaging the world in the manner that brings us joy. But around age seven, the negative voices of the world begin infiltrating our innocent brains. However, some truly brave souls have the capacity to keep wearing their red rain boots whether anyone else thinks that's appropriate footwear. For the rest of us, at some point we begin to let our true voice be drowned out by the noise of the world around us. We begin to doubt the importance of our authenticity. We trade in our red rain boots for what others would have us wear.

It doesn't have to stay that way. Somewhere, in the back of your mind's closet, are your version of red rain boots. Remember when you felt the most authentic version of you? It was pretty awesome, wasn't it? You can go there again, and this time, you will have the wisdom gained from your experience and knowledge. It's as simple as looking in the mirror. Look closely. Lean in. Look into those one-of-a-kind eyes looking back at you and say out loud, "Hey, I know you. I've missed you."

Make space to put down your phone, close the laptop and turn off the television to spend some time with *you*. Get to know you again. You'll have a great time reconnecting. Share your favorite memories and any surprises from your journey of discovery with a friend. Read this book together. Share your Pause and Practice exercises if it's helpful. Listen to what your red rain boots are telling you. *"Go farther."* It's what you're meant to do.

As a special gift, take my What's Your Inner Critic's Personality Type Quiz: www.calmyourinnercritic/quiz. It's short, simple, and rooted in personality science and will give us another opportunity to deepen your understanding of all things- You.

Settle in and turn the page. It's time to find the howl of your whisper.

I'm right here beside you, cheering you on.

1

THE WAKE-UP
CALL OF MY LIFE

From Aimless to Authentic

"You won't do it! You chicken! You won't do it!," my younger brother, Adam, taunted. He stood at the bottom of the giant stone steps of our front porch, sneering up at me.

The dare was to jump from the very top step to the grass beyond the bottom step. The drop was about eight feet, but it might as well have been eight hundred feet from my eleven-year-old perspective. Back then, most everything seemed out of my reach. No one ever picked me for teams at recess; I was skinny, awkward, and a major nerd. I remember asking one of the cool kids at school what they thought of the poem "Hiawatha" by Henry Longfellow and what was his favorite stanza. He gaped at me like I had two heads. Yep. Nerd alert.

My brother's heckling reminded me of all of it. So, I was determined to prove him wrong. Determined to land at the bottom of the steps, standing directly in front of his sneering face. That'd shut him up.

I took a deep breath, crouched low, teeth clenched, and leapt forward as mightily as I could. As my feet slid out from under me on the damp grass, my head barely cleared the bottom step. I hit the ground with a hard *thud* that forced the air out of my lungs. It was as if someone was suffocating me. I lay there gasping as my brother stood over me in peals of triumphant laughter. And a voice inside my head was laughing at me just as hard.

Thirty-five years later, just past midnight, the telephone next to the hospital bed rang. The voice on the other end said, "This is Dr. Puri. I wanted to call you myself with the results." Then came a pause—you know, that pause that feels like a decade.

"Your daughter has had a stroke." I didn't hear another word. His voice faded into the whirs and beeps of the machines. I looked over at my beautiful, sleeping 16-year-old daughter, Annemarie. I reached for her hand, and the air left my lungs just as sharply as that day when I was a kid laid out flat in the yard. And again, I was gasping for my next breath.

For reasons no one to this day can explain, my daughter survived a vertebral artery dissection and the stroke that followed the next day when a small blood clot broke loose and traveled to her brain stem. The medical team that cared for her referred to her as their miracle girl. When describing the 1-in-a-million fluke event she experienced, her neurologist told her she was "the luckiest, unlucky girl in the world." The remnants of the stroke are minuscule in comparison to what could have been her future. Today, she has a career she loves and has given me a wonderful son-in-law (son-in-love as we call him), two beautiful little granddaughters, and a grandson on the way.

After the stroke, I was reminded often of her miracle while seated in the pediatric neurology waiting room with other parents and children whose lives had been forever altered. I knew she was indeed a miracle.

I thought of how close I'd come to losing my daughter on the day of her junior prom, less than a year after her stroke. She was stunning, and "he" was on the way with a corsage in hand. Months later, I'd learn why she'd been hysterical over a last-minute repair to her gown. She feared it would make them late to meet up with their friends. "You don't understand! You just don't understand!," she wailed.

She was right. I hadn't a clue.

We'd been in family counseling since the stroke to learn how to move forward in a healthy way after a life-threatening event with a teenager. The therapist educated us that it's not uncommon to "infantilize" a child out of a desire to protect them. I understood that problem. When she came home from the hospital, I wanted to sleep in her bed with her. When her dad vetoed that, I suggested putting a video baby monitor in her room. "No" was, again, the answer.

The road to her recovery was bumpy. I read everything I could on brain neuroplasticity and discovered workarounds as she adapted during the healing process. Her doctors and therapists confirmed that new pathways were generating at a remarkable rate, leaving little trace of the damage intended by the stroke.

She was happy to be dating a young man from the high school football team. Things were going well… At first. As time went on, something seemed off. Tears after phone calls. My intuition said this was beyond nerves, puppy love, and teenage emotions. I was labeled an "overreacting mom." Maybe she was right. Would I have been so preoccupied with every move she made if the stroke had never happened?

Her junior year of high school was on track, and she was doing well. Her therapist was pleased with her progress and informed us it was usual for emotions to be dysregulated as the brain healed from an injury; irritability, moodiness, weepiness. In a moment of scarce levity in those days, I remarked, it didn't sound different than normal teenage girldom. Once again, I didn't have a clue. During a counseling session a few months later, with the encouragement of her astute therapist, my brave daughter finally told me that she was in an abusive relationship.

When the story came tumbling out amid her sobs, the air left my lungs once again. But in the days following the nightmarish revelation, I didn't feel suffocated. My voice wasn't stolen this time. I found my voice. I found me, and I'd been looking for me my whole life. My spirit howled one, single, deafening word:

"Enough!"

While the injury from the stroke had terrified me, the violation of my daughter's mind, body, and spirit awakened a powerful primal and Divine instinct. A howl began to rise from deep within. The whisper of my own soul I'd been stifling for decades rose. This time it refused to be silenced. It grew louder, stronger. I'd finally had *enough*.

I couldn't accept the status quo anymore. The crisis with my teenage daughter brought me to my knees mentally, emotionally, spiritually, and physically; that was the wake-up call of my life. I could either continue down the road I was traveling, or, in the immortal words of Robert Frost, "Take the road less traveled." Thank you, Robert. I, too, "chose the latter, and it made all the difference." I was jolted out of the complacency to which I'd become accustomed. Something inside me had a message. But what was it that seemed so close and yet so far out of my grasp? I'd forgotten the sound of my own truth. Did I ever know it? I needed a hero to rescue me.

The experience with my daughter left me in desperate need of a lifeline, so I considered my strengths from a more holistic perspective, not just as a career booster, but as a tool for all aspects of my life. People who consciously aim their strengths consistently are three times more likely to report an excellent quality of life. Even before my daughter's situation, I was missing the mark in that department. I wanted to know how I could move forward in living my life in a way that felt true to me by embracing what made me unique and strong enough to live that way. So, I put my strengths into practice in my everyday life.

While writing this book, I had the wind knocked out of me again. This wasn't a losing my footing kind of experience or even a gasping for air kind of scenario. This was a sledgehammer to the chest. Had I not done the earlier work regarding all that broke loose during my daughter's recovery, I wouldn't have had the wisdom, the grit, or the self-compassion to make it through the hell of a journey I'm coming through. (I'll share that story in the next book).

Rocking Chair Regret

About a year after my "enough" awakening, I was sitting on my screened porch reading a magazine and came across an article on "rocking chair regrets." Which do you think you would regret more in old age: 1) living your authentic truth even when others disapprove; or 2) living life doing what you think you *should* do?

If you could start life over again, what would you do differently?

People over sixty-five years old revealed their regrets in a research study conducted by a group of Canadian health researchers, and the results may surprise you. The participants were asked: "If you could start life over again, what would you do differently?" Three themes emerged. The respondents answered that they would have:

1. Set aside time for reflection on a regular basis
2. Made more courageous choices
3. Been more purposeful and selective in how they spent their time and energy

The answers revealed regrets around not acknowledging, trusting, and following their inner truth.

Reflecting on the article, I sat back in my chair, took a deep breath, and really asked myself, *Am I living a life that is mindful, intentional, courageous, and grounded in authenticity*? I was doing "good stuff" at the helm of a leadership development nonprofit by then, but I couldn't say that work was truly fulfilling to my spirit, nor was it always being carried out with a cheerful heart. I didn't know if my choices matched my definition of success; not what the world said was success: keeping up with the Joneses and imitating life portrayed in slick advertising. What genuine success looked like for me. As ridiculous as this sounds to me now, I wasn't even sure defining success was up to me.

I swallowed hard. A half-embarrassed, half-alarmed feeling of chagrin swept over me, and I realized the raw truth. I couldn't define what genuine success meant for me. All the definitions I'd been programmed to believe came flooding to the forefront. *Successful people live like this, drive this, eat this, have this job, have this much money…* My brain ran in a frenzy to and fro picking the lowest hanging fruit, offering it up, asking, "Is this it? How about this?" Not only could I not pinpoint what my definition was, but it was becoming clearer that what others had convinced me meant success wasn't right either. Worse than that: I didn't have a clue how to choose for myself.

Until this article, I never considered that I *could* choose. Now I saw that I must. The remainder of my very existence depended on it. I needed to grab on to something, anything, that felt "right." Right to the world's definition *and* right to me. There had to be a way to have both.

I thought about what I'd done in my life that brought my deepest sense of accomplishment. Was it education? Work? Being a good spouse? An important cause I'd worked on? These things brought approval, accomplishments, and accolades. But had they given me a sense of higher meaning? Produced in me a sense of genuine success in *my one life*? I felt little alignment between my life's pursuits and my life purpose.

Then came the clincher—motherhood? Many women would say motherhood. I'm blessed to be a mother, and I'm very proud of my three amazing children, Kyle, John Paul, and Annemarie. But I always felt I could've been a better mother. Even in that role, my authenticity was hijacked by others' expectations, and I hadn't possessed the courage to stand up to them.

I closed my eyes in meditation and pictured my eighty-five-year-old self in the rocking chair across from present-day me. My white

Don't wait. Be bold. Find your courage.

hair is fixed in a twist, and I'm still wearing stylish glasses. I ask her, "If no one else were looking, what would a life of purpose and fulfillment look like for me?"

"Don't wait," she whispers. "Be bold," she urges with a slight mischievous grin. "Find your courage," she implores with her eyes twinkling.

Her words spoke directly to forty-seven-year-old me. I leaned toward her, tongue-tied with all the questions I wanted to ask.

"Promise us you'll do it," she said. I nodded as if in a trance. "And meet us here without—" Then she vanished into the mist of my mind's eye.

"Wait! Without what?!" There was no reply. I came back from meditation blinking and feeling a little confused.

I knew she was there in the distance, waiting for me to fulfill the promise. *What was I to present (and not present) to my eighty-five-year-old self?* I wish this was the part where I tell you about the epiphany I had. What I did have was no idea. The words that haunted me the most weren't what I expected, but rang true and deep, "Don't wait." At that time of my life, I was pulled in what felt like a million different directions. I was exhausted and unfulfilled. The face staring back in the mirror asked, "How did you get up here? You don't even want to do most of the things you do."

What was I not supposed to bring to my future self? I found a clue while reading an old favorite, *The Alchemist* by Paul Coelho: "Maybe the journey isn't so much about becoming anything. Maybe it's about unbecoming everything that isn't really you, so you can be who you were meant to be in the first place." The words veritably glowed on the page. *Was that her point*? Instead of searching for more, better, new, and different aspects of myself that reflected my personal definition of living a successful life, perhaps she wanted me to meet her at eighty-five without anything that wasn't authentic.

The me I'd known and always believed myself to be was: me, a product of date-rape; me, given away because my birth wasn't acceptable; me, sexually abused and silenced; me, living for approval through awards, ribbons, and trophies; me, climbing the ever elusive mountain of perfectionism; me, following all of the rules of religion while hearing I'd always fall short; me, starving to make my body disappear to match my unseen soul; me, battling the demons of anxiety, depression; me, depending on prescriptions as answers; me, failing to follow my intuition in mothering my children.

Maybe it's about unbecoming everything that isn't really you

What if my eighty-five-year-old self meant that none of those things were my Authentic Me? Certainly, they were parts of my life experience, but they weren't the definition of me. That was all my inner critic's doing.

Now, don't get jealous. You've got an inner critic, too. So, just what is the inner critic, and how did you get lucky enough to have one of your very own? The *Webster's Merriam-Webster* dictionary tells us that a critic is "one who judges, evaluates, or criticizes. One who tends too readily to make captious, trivial, or harsh judgments. A faultfinder." Inner, of course, is simply that which is inside.

Your inner critic is a faultfinder that lives within you. *Terrific*. Not only do you have a world full of judgmental voices, an obnoxious magpie symphony, telling you what, when, where, why, and how you should live in order to be acceptable, even when you try to shut the door and lock out the world's opinions… But your very own personal judge is poised and waiting in the mirror, ready to find fault with every word, thought, and deed.

Believe it or not, that's actually very good news for you and me. This internal 'judge' is not a true judge. In my personal walk of faith, there's only One. The One. Jehovah Jireh is the One who sees, loves, accepts, and provides for us. I came to know that Truth through Christ. Whether my belief aligns with the God of your understanding, or you're agnostic, atheist, or seeking, the most important thing I want you to know is that the internal judge whispering in your ear is an imposter. The word "imposter" comes from the Latin *imponere,* which means "to deceive, impose, or inflict." And that, my fine, courageous friend, is exactly how your inner critic leads you into imposter syndrome, searching for external ways to feign worthiness.

I spent my life trying to cover my wounds with the band-aids of applause, trophies, and awards based on what others valued. My inner critic deceived me time and again, saying, "This is it. Everyone will know you're really something after this." I bought into the lie that acceptance and fulfillment were just around the corner of my next success. I'd give my all, reach the pinnacle, and still be netted by imposter syndrome, drowning in doubt and fear. Another ocean was always waiting for me. This existence was exhausting. I'd swim hard like a trumpetfish (trumpetfish swim closely with other fish to conceal their true identity) to prove that I fit in, only to live trapped by fear that I'd be found out to be a fake.

The event with my daughter cut my voice loose from where my inner critic had trapped it. Then, my eighty-five-year-old self screamed, "Enough," setting me free to be the hero in the story of *my* life. Fortunately, I had a role model to follow.

The Hero I Deserved (Towanda)

I love the movie *Fried Green Tomatoes* starring Kathy Bates. In fact, I love everything Kathy Bates. She's a creative genius, and I feel a kind of thespian kinship with her. She got her start at Actors Theatre of Louisville in Kentucky, just up the road from the theatre company I've been a part of since 2011. Anyway, Kathy's character, Evelyn, finally has enough of being treated like an invisible doormat. She channels "Towanda," her alter-ego, and empowers herself to be seen and heard for the first time in her life. In striking a blow for her newfound freedom, she takes a sledgehammer to a wall in her dark home and allows the sunlight to come flooding in. Emboldened, she makes a "striking" impression on some mean girls in the grocery store parking lot, which in my humble opinion is the Best. Scene. Ever.

The traumas my daughter endured unleashed my own "Towanda." The clarity of what I wanted and deserved began to come into focus. I was getting crystal clear on what I didn't want my life to be anymore. Towanda was in the house. She'd been there all along, waiting for me year after year as I'd allowed myself to be muzzled. She gently but firmly whispered how I'd swallowed my dreams and silenced my truth to keep others happy. Pretending to be someone I wasn't to please people who weren't interested in knowing the "real me." But then again, neither was I. At some point that I hadn't even noticed, the proverbial muzzle others had placed on me wasn't even a required apparatus anymore. I silenced myself quite effectively. Effortlessly. Then Towanda put her foot down: *There'll be no more settling for less than we were created to be.*

There'll be no more settling for less than we were created to be.

I became more aware of what I was allowing. I noticed one Saturday evening my stomach began cramping, and a nagging headache began. By the next morning, I had a full-on migraine. My daughter's much better-suited boyfriend (now my son-in-love) made an off-hand joke about how many times I was missing church. He said, "Funny how every Sunday you have a headache before church." He was right. Every Sunday. The night before, I began feeling tense and unwell, and each Sunday morning, I woke up with a migraine. Sometimes, feeling guilty, I made myself go to be a "good Christian." Other times, I just couldn't.

I went to church to feel close to God, give thanks and praise, and hear a message to help me live my life the right way. Yet, each Sunday, I felt worse. Disconnected. Discouraged. I remember my last Sunday morning inside a church building. I was sobbing. Heaving sobbing. Church was supposed to make me feel better. Be my refuge. My answer. But church was none of those things. Wasn't that what God's unconditional love… Why Christ came… Where we're meant to find genuine acceptance… My heart was in a twister of inconsistency.

Thoughts flooded my mind. If all that was true, but unconditional love and acceptance weren't for me, then what was wrong with me? Why wasn't church working for me? Since my teen years, when I was alone in the woods or in my room, I would write my deepest thoughts and prayers, wanting to know more about the loving Creator on a personal level. However, the dogma I'd long sat under of legalism, judgment, and harshness eventually choked out the love I knew I should feel in my heart, soul, mind, and body. I had become a harsh and critical person. My inner critic feasted on these delicacies, which were never in short supply. Much of the time, I perceived how others were thinking or behaving incorrectly, and there was my inner critic hissing in my ear how I was right, and they were wrong.

Sitting in my seat that final day with the worship songs blaring and my heart pounding, I recognized that for many people, 'religion' is a meaningful part of their spiritual journey and deeply connects them to their faith. That it's right for them. Amidst my sobs, I also realized that for me, religion was a box. It kept me confined to a world of do's and don'ts, separating me from the gift of freedom and the love of and for God. Wasn't I in the right place to find those things? More sobs came as I prayed, "What's happening to me? What's wrong? How do I…?"

From the deepest recesses of my spirit, I heard, "I'm not here."

If I wasn't going to find God inside those four walls, I'd have to discover where I would. I was dangerously close to sleepwalking off a cliff into the abyss of acquiescence. Half of my life was behind me. *What was I waiting for?*

The pain I was in, emotionally, spiritually, and physically, had grown from a whisper to a howl I couldn't ignore. So, I gathered my courage to smash through the walls just like Towanda.

My inner critic was ready and waiting. She sneered; *You don't have real faith. You're a backslider and everyone will know it if you stop going to church. You're not a real Christian.* Her hiss was deafening, taking her strength from my hell, fire, and brimstone upbringing with reinforcement from my rigid adult religious experiences. While they'd been more polished in their delivery, they were just as effective in their controlling legalism. All my life that judgmental voice had me on a leash—ready to yank me back in line at the first sign of dissent.

I stood up straight, picked up my sledge-hammer, and knocked a hole through my judgmental inner critic to let in the light of authentic me. Towanda slapped me on the back, popped her chewing gum and said, "Listen to your authentic voice and tell the others to sit down and shut up." So, I chose the real, unvarnished, imperfect, *me*. My duty—no, my honor—was to give voice to the girl who'd been waiting for someone to hear her, to see her.

The following Friday, I decided I wouldn't go to the church house on Sunday. And an unexpected thing happened. There were no Saturday night stomach cramps, nor a Sunday morning migraine. I felt….light. I enjoyed and felt nourished in my personal worship, enjoying the Sabbath for the first time in a long time. My authentic self, the one I'd ignored my entire life, told me, "This is the Way."

She led me to tackle the difficult inner child and inner critic work. Fighting to put my inner critic in its place was essential to revealing my authentic self and my God-given purpose. I perceived how my inner critic was, essentially, fighting with God over Their creation—*me*.

You've Always Had the Power, My Dear

The tug-of-war between my inner critic and my authentic self often feels like the struggle between Glinda, The Good Witch, and the Wicked Witch of the West. Have you ever felt lost and powerless, as if a tornado dumped you into a maze, like something right out of *The Wizard of Oz*? The film version still runs on late-night cable, and I watch it over and over. The story can hit a chord deep within us where we've felt lost and confused; felt we weren't as smart as others; wanted to love and have someone to genuinely love us; wished we had more courage in certain circumstances; and we've all known someone acting "witchy"—or *maybe we were the witch*. I'll plead the fifth on that one. How fortunate we were when we found "Glinda" in our lives. A guide to help us see our strengths.

There's a part of the story, though, that always used to make me angry. At the end of the movie, everyone has their wish. The Scarecrow has a brain, the Tin Man receives his heart, and the Lion is filled with courage. While Dorothy is happy for her friends, she's still lost, confused, and just wants to go home. *What about her wish?*

That's when the beautiful Good Witch leans in and tells Dorothy, "You've always had the power, my dear. You just had to learn it for yourself."

I must mention that during most of the movie, Dorothy wears these incredible ruby red shoes that she may or may not have 'acquired' from the deceased Wicked Witch of the East, but let's not get bogged down in minor details of property rights. Let's face it: They were killer shoes. Pardon the pun. Ask anyone who knows me about my shoe obsession, and you'll know that Dorothy was a girl after my own heart. Shoes, especially *red shoes*, get me every time... But I digress.

The point is—like it or not—Glinda was right. Dorothy always had the power to find her way home. She had the shoes, and she had her voice. So, she clicked her heels together three times and said, "There's no place like home, there's no place like home, there's no place like home." Suddenly, she opens her eyes and is surrounded by all the love she thought she'd lost.

You, too, have all the strength of your unique brain, heart, and brand of courage to find your way home—to find your way back to Authentic You, like Dorothy's trip down the yellow brick road. There'll be forests of twists and turns, fields of poppies that will lull you into complacency, thunderstorms, sunny skies, along with guides, allies, challengers, as well as the occasional flying monkey you could have never seen coming. Commit to locking arms with a trustworthy traveling companion or two. Before you know it, you'll be well on your way.

This book is a stepping stone on your yellow brick road, and I'm your traveling companion for this part of your journey. Acknowledge your inner wisdom. Find your way to fearless, Authentic You. So, when your inner critic pipes up and says you're not smart enough, brave enough, or they don't like you, or the dozens of other lies it spouts as you allow it to flit around inside your head, know this. *Not True.* Not a word of it. You're a uniquely intelligent child of God. Because of this, you have compassion in your strong heart and are braver than you think.

Look how far you've already come. Getting a wake-up call to your life from your inner voice is like being sucked into a tornado and gaining consciousness in the Land of Oz. Finding your way back home to your authentic self requires you to decide what truly matters to you and fight for it like Towanda. Fortunately, you've had the power to win this battle all along. To find your ruby red slippers—that is, your inner strengths—we first have to return to the origins of your inner critic, which is the focus of Chapter 2.

Becoming familiar with the steps for success on this new journey you're embarking on is important. So I've set up a simple way for you to work with the concepts in each chapter to reinforce your progress as you move through the pages that follow.

Meet me at Pause & Practice for Chapter 1 in the back of the book.

2

THE INNER CRITIC'S ORIGINS

The Safety of Staying Silent

I bet you have a pivotal story of getting the wind knocked out of you. You've listened to your inner critic that denied your strengths and obscured your self-clarity that you knew at your core to be true. In doing so, you turned your authentic voice, the one that wants to howl with your inner truth, down to barely above laryngitis. You've lived life on other people's terms by rules and conditions you didn't set up, in the name of protecting yourself. *And none of it is your fault.*

Giving in to your inner critic is especially understandable considering how young you likely were when your authentic voice was first challenged. It appeared with the answers to keep you safe, and all it asked in return was that you make room for it. It began to take up more space, then more. There began an odd feeling of safety, knowing that as you were needed to put yourself out there less and less, your voice wasn't that important. And there you were with a full-blown case of inner truth laryngitis.

Your authentic voice is still there. I promise. You heard it when you decided to read this book. That raspy whisper's growing louder. It knows you've passed the point of excuses for not calling the inner critic's lies into the open to defeat them. The Authentic You demands some tender loving care. And if whispering isn't working, it may choose to assault your senses with a painful shriek demanding you to give your authentic self the attention it's been desperately begging for.

No matter where you are on this journey—whether you're listening to those early whispers, or you've noticed that whisper getting louder, or, like me, you ignored the howl until unbearable pain accompanied it to get your attention—you're here now. You get to choose the form your authentic voice takes: Freedom or Forbiddance. Instead of shrinking, keeping your head down, staying off the radar, and doing the next mundane thing in front of you, you can allow your inner truth to speak.

Clients ready to listen sometimes ask, "How do I recognize my authentic voice? Some days I don't even know who I am."

It's waiting for you right where you left it—in your origin story.

Find Your Voice in Your Story

This part of your journey may very well be the most difficult. It's certainly been the most difficult part of this book to write. To go back to the origins of my inner critic. But it's a bridge I had to cross. You have your bridge to cross. Honor this sacred part of your journey toward your highest self. The living in authenticity part. It's where you'll find your unapologetic howl for the life you deserve. The life you were created for from the beginning of time.

There was a time before you knew your inner critic. A time when you didn't have to prove yourself. A time when you were happy to simply be alive in your skin. So, what happened? What changed to make you believe that being you wasn't good enough? Your clarity of who you were created to be was clouded. Someone or *someones* got inside your head and hijacked the truth. They disrupted your confidence in expressing your true self. Your true voice became smaller and quieter, while the negative voice got larger and louder. Other people didn't need to silence your voice anymore; your inner critic began handling that.

Fortunately, no matter what's happened in your life, you can know the real you. The one you were created to be. The one and only you. The person you would've been if "it" hadn't happened. Don't let who you know you really are remain a distant memory. Recovering your authentic self involves shedding your inner critic's fake version of you. Crossing to the 'authentic you' side of the bridge, you may be tempted to look back across the chasm. It's familiar back there. Ahead lies uncharted territory. Remember, what you don't change, you condone. What you condone, you accept. Don't retreat into past stories. That's

> **Recovering your authentic self involves shedding your inner critic's fake version of you.**

your inner critic raising its voice to scare you back into the brambles where it's taught you it's safer than out in the open. Look at your compass and keep going.

My Story

During my personal healing work, the origin of my inner critic surfaced. From the beginning, it had told me I wasn't wanted. I don't remember ever not feeling like there was some 'invisible something' wrong with me. But others sensed it, and some turned away or felt entitled to hurt me.

I was a very little girl when I lost my authentic voice. I was the product of date rape of a college student who placed me for adoption. After a year in foster care, primarily left in a crib, my developmental needs had been mostly ignored. I didn't crawl well, nor was I attempting to stand or talk. My adopted parents had waited nine years for a child, and, oh, how they loved me. They couldn't have imagined that by the time I was three and a half, an extended family member would betray them, and my needs would be sacrificed again.

Although I went to my new mom smilingly, Dad remembers something was "off" from the beginning. Aside from barely crawling or trying to stand, I never cried. Ever. After about six weeks into the adoption trial period, it was mentioned to the visiting social worker. She said, "Babies, like Mary, left in a crib learn that crying doesn't get them anywhere, so eventually they stop." The flattened area on the back of my head seemed to support her theory.

Eventually, I did cry, but doing so was never something I put much stock in as worthwhile. The years would continue to prove it wasn't useful. When I cried, it seemed to frustrate people, particularly if I didn't immediately stop after being told to. Crying was soon filed away to the back of my brain in the "Things People Don't Want to Hear from Me" drawer.

For most of my life, I accepted that insurmountable circumstances beyond my control had dictated a path for me. While I've always known I was adopted, my parents never referred to me as their "adopted" daughter, and they wanted me to understand it as a wonderful thing. I even had a special hardcover book about all the wonderful things being adopted meant. Mom explained the "nice lady" who gave birth to me couldn't take care of me, so she made sure I'd have a mommy and daddy who could. All the other mothers had to take whatever baby the hospital gave them. But I had been specially chosen.

As a small girl, I told myself that my parents adopted me because nine years is a long time to wait for a baby. So, they had to "settle" for me because there weren't any newborns, and I had this inherent flaw I was sure they could see. *Beggars can't be choosers, ya know.*

In my late thirties, during a renewed search for my birth mother, I discovered that three other couples had turned me down. There was a concern of hydrocephalus at birth when my head diameter measured a ¼" larger than my chest. At six months old, I was completely cleared by the Chief of Pediatrics at the University of

Kentucky, but the information remained in my medical records. Most adoptive parents weren't willing to take the risk.

When I shared the social work file with my parents, my mother became upset that anyone wouldn't think I was the most perfect baby. My dad snickered and gently reminded her that if any of the other couples had, they wouldn't have me. She sheepishly grinned, nodded, but added, "It still makes me mad."

The bottom line seemed to me to be that before you can be "chosen," someone has to *not* want you. Someone discards you. That part of adoption wasn't so wonderful. By age 1, I'd been given away by my birth mother and presented like a new puppy to three other couples who decided, "We'll pass. Have you got anything else?" Of course, I don't consciously remember any of it. But subconsciously, I received the whispers of rejection loud and clear.

As a child who had her beginning in a year of foster care, I had a recurring dream that I was amongst a row of babies in high chairs placed in a storefront window. We were gumming on carrots with leafy, green tops. People passed by, waved, and made silly faces. Sometimes the bell on the shop door jingled as some came in. There'd be laughing and cooing. The bell would jingle again, resulting in an empty high chair and abandoned carrot. No one ever cooed over me in the dream, reinforcing my belief that I didn't measure up.

Acquired Silence

We will sacrifice our authentic voices to please those we love most because we desperately need their love in return. This seems particularly true for our mothers. What a labyrinth we stumble through to stay in their good graces. I don't have to tell most of the women reading this that the relationship between mother and daughter can be complicated. Mine certainly was, and for decades, my inner critic made the most of it.

My mother was loving and stern. There was little margin for error. The constant presence of low-grade anxiety, not to say or do the wrong thing, was a normal part of life. Now and then, I'd try to share something that one of my friends had done or said, or share a point of view when I got up the courage to express my opinion. Each time, her response would be to shake her head, chuckle a little, and say, "Silly yung'un." Then I was dismissed for more important tasks about the house, or my words invited a lecture on how my friend's behavior or my way of thinking was wrong.

Mom had high standards. Those standards imprinted integrity, a strong work ethic, and a desire for excellence within me. She believed in personal accountability and responsibility. You didn't question or challenge her beliefs or authority. It wouldn't surprise me if she had Belief®, Command®, and Self-Assurance® in her Top 5. That's a powerful combination positively and negatively depending on which side the coin lands that day.

Good memories flood my mind when I think of Mom, too. Teaching me to cook and sew. Standing on the back porch every time my brother, Adam, and I came home from a 4-H competition, she was ready to hug us whether we brought back the champion ribbon or not. She loved literature and was an undocumented genius, graduating high school at barely fifteen (would've been fourteen, had she not had to repeat the fourth grade due to a long bout of whooping cough). She ordered by mail and worked the most difficult expert level of Dell® crossword puzzle books—in ink.

During her later years, when she was diagnosed with global vascular dementia, the doctor said her high IQ helped her to mask symptoms and work around things for years before we began noticing the signs. The dementia diagnosis was horrible, yet as the disease progressed, her personality softened. Close to the end, she began to be almost child-like at times. I had never been able to be authentic with her, and now she wanted nothing more than to connect with me. And we couldn't. She forgot my name at times. Dementia robbed her of the capacity to comprehend even close to her previous level. One of the great sadnesses of my life is never being able to share the whispers of my soul with her.

Voiceless

After my mother died in 2018, I was determined to remember only the good things. That wasn't so easy. *Don't speak or think ill of the dead* kept running through my mind. *She did the best she could.* My grief rose in unexpected ways. Resentment at how she'd handled me growing up began to surface. Things I thought I'd put to rest were pricking at me again. I couldn't ignore the unwelcome howl that was rising. I felt like a horrible, ungrateful daughter.

The main issue surrounded the handling of my childhood sexual abuse by an extended family member. It began around age three and a half and wouldn't end until I was almost eleven. Seven years. Sharing particulars isn't important, but the abuse and messaging from my abuser reinforced in my child's brain that I was defective. Why else would I have been "chosen" unless I had no value? I began to feel non-existent.

We'd return home from a family get-together, and I'd lie awake in bed, softly crying to myself. My cries would get a little louder, "Mommy. Mom." I'd envision her hearing me. She would get up, put on her pretty pink housecoat with the embroidered blue flowers, then walk down the long hallway into my room. My fantasy would continue with her taking me into her arms, and without me saying a word, she would "know." She'd hold me close, stroke my hair, kiss the top of my head, and tell me I'd done nothing wrong. That I'd never have to see him again. And as she smiled down at me and told me she loved me, the pain would all go away.

But that never happened. When my crying was loud enough that I might actually be heard, I'd realize that if she came, she wouldn't just "know." I'd have to tell her. Me. With my voice. Tell her the atrocities. His cajoling words and hissing threats flooded my child's brain: I was convinced my parents would assume his behavior was my fault. I'd be told I was in the wrong. There'd be no benefit of the doubt. I was, after all, defective. My birth mother had seen it, now my abuser, and if I told, my adopted mom would realize it, too.

One time at about age eight, I threatened to "tell." Without pause, he smugly said that all the family knew I was a liar. Mom had told her sister about my lying at school. No one would believe me over him, the adult. I knew he was right. As a child, I lied a lot. I made up stories about my real parents dying in a fiery car crash, leaving me an orphan. I lied to get out of trouble. That just led to being in more trouble. My abuser knew all of this. His threat worked. *For a while.*

Experiences that quiet our voice don't occur in isolation. They become recordings that your inner critic keeps at the ready to replay over and over. Your very own Top 40 hits. You believe them even more deeply when others reinforce them through idle comments or gossip. When you're not mindful of the internal manipulation, the lies root themselves, and you unwittingly accept them as facts. Your negativity-seeking inner critic digs deeper and deeper into your psyche until you hear its voice first every time. When you give greater weight to another's opinion of you than to your authentic self's knowledge of you, you're an active participant in giving your power away. But you can always take it back.

Experiences that quiet our voice don't occur in isolation.

By age nine, I'd gotten better at dodging him. One afternoon, as I tried to make my way back down past him after he'd quietly crept up the stairs, he became very frustrated in his attempt to corner me like a mouse. We were often sent to play upstairs in their attic loft, where an old toybox was kept. Finally, he stopped and took a long drag on his cigarette. "Fine. If that's the way you want it," he said in a low voice. He took a knee, gazed out the little window, and looked at me. He smiled, then looked out the window again as a bigger smile crossed his face. He said, "Just fine." Then he went downstairs.

I went to the window and looked out. My heart froze in terror at the sight. Adam was playing under a peach tree in the backyard. My stomach twisted in a knot. And I made my choice.

Whisper Snuffed Out

Over the next year, the visits back and forth seemed more than usual. I began to withdraw, not wanting to be hugged or even touched by anyone. I would go into the front room of our house with the "good furniture," where we weren't allowed to play, and sit curled up with a quilt on the end of the couch and get lost in my books. Sometimes my mother would find me just staring out the big picture window. She'd tell me to stop moping and find a chore for me to do.

Shortly after another visit, I was staring out the window, trapped deep in my thoughts. I didn't hear her when she sat down next to me and touched my shoulder. I recoiled. Our eyes locked. She saw the terror. Her face froze.

And I knew… she knew.

She said with a frog in her throat, "Is someone, *ahem,* 'bothering' you? If someone's bothering you, you can tell me." So, I began to try. I squeaked out the first tiny bits of information. As I spoke, her face grew red, her lips pursed, and her eyes became moist as the blue vein in her temple began to bulge. She put her hand on mine and thought it best if I went up to my room to lie down for a while. I was glad for the break. I couldn't get the words out, didn't know how to say what was happening to me, and there was more I'd have to tell. I was unbelievably exhausted from the few words I had managed to squeak out. I dozed off to the sounds of my mother starting supper.

I woke to murmuring voices down in the kitchen. As I heard my dad's footsteps on the stairs, it suddenly dawned on me that he would have to know, too. My dad was my everything. I trusted him completely. He was never harsh or disapproving of me. But now he would know the "terrible awful" I'd been hiding. (Right up there with Kathy Bates is Octavia Spencer and her breathtaking role in *The Help*).

He'll never look at me the same again, I thought. He sat on the edge of my bed peeling an orange, his favorite snack. For years after this encounter, I could barely tolerate the smell of citrus. One way I knew I was truly healing from the trauma of my sexual abuse was that I began to enjoy the scent and taste of oranges again. That may seem trivial, but oranges were a turning point in my recovery. Citrus is now one of my favorite scents.

He asked me to tell him what I'd told Mom. I kept my gaze on the orange, unable to look at him. His hands peeling away the skin like I'd seen him do dozens of times before when we'd share the snack. As confessing what had been happening got harder, I closed my eyes tight. The smell of citrus grew stronger. I opened my eyes to see the orange squeezed to mush in my father's hand, juice running down his fingers onto my bedspread. He was stone silent. The color had left his face. Through a clenched jaw, he croaked out the words, "That's enough. You don't have to say anymore." And he left.

I heard a small commotion downstairs. The little broom closet door opened and closed hard. I could hear my mother saying my dad's name over and over, pleading with him to "listen to reason." I crept down the narrow staircase and peeked around the corner. My mother's back was against the kitchen door, blocking my father from exiting with the rifle in his hands. "What good will it do her if you spend the rest of your life in prison?" He hung his head, set the rifle down, and they held each other and cried.

I knew I could never speak about what had happened again. If I ever told the whole story, my father would kill my abuser and go to prison—and it would be my fault. *My voice could destroy my family.*

In the weeks that followed, my mother would try to talk with me about what had happened to me, but I would break down into hysterics. My parents saw a psychiatrist for guidance. He told them I was young; nothing had really happened other than some fondling back and forth, and in time, I would forget anything had ever happened. They considered having my abuser arrested but learned that I'd be required to testify in open court. This was a standard practice of the judicial system in the 1970s. My hysterics became worse at any mention of the subject, so it was never discussed again. There were no more visits. I didn't go to family reunions where he'd be. No more trips to my grandparents if he was going to be around, and it would never be spoken of to them. It might give them a heart attack was the general fear.

But. Yes, there's a but. When I turned 14, my mother felt it was time to "get on with things" and announced I'd be going back to the family reunion that year. I pleaded, but her mind was made up. She had a pull yourself up by the bootstraps mindset. And so I went. And there he was. My skin crawled. I felt like I couldn't breathe. I had begged my dad not to let her make me go. All to no avail. Oh, they watched him like a hawk. They kept him at a distance, but that didn't matter. He was still inside my head. And the smirk on his face told me he knew it, too.

I felt dismissed and devalued—again. The difference this time was that I knew my parents had made a conscious decision to put aside what I wanted, in favor of quieting inquiring cousins, aunts, and grandparents asking why I didn't come with them to the reunion anymore. The negative voice in my head grew louder in its criticism. *Nothing could ever erase the defect I was.* There was something inherently wrong with me. I wanted to disappear. I suppose that's when the anorexia began.

The Howl I Finally Heeded

Psychological damage followed me into adulthood, leading me on an endless quest to discover my identity at a core level. As a young woman, from the outside, a lot of my life looked rosy; achievements and accolades through activities where one could prove worth through award ribbons, trophies, and medals. But at the core, it was all a sham, and I felt like a phony. If they *really* knew me... they'd run. I couldn't keep blaming my birth mother, how I was conceived, foster care, my adopted family, or any other horrible circumstances. So, I just accepted that I was damaged and tried to pull myself up by the bootstraps. It was too late to know or be who I was supposed to have been if my life had had a better start.

I was the skinny, flat-chested girl who was the butt of all the "toothpick" and "IBTC" (Itty Bitty Titty Committee) jokes at school. By the time I was 21, I'd been married for about 18 months and living across the country in Washington State. Keith was in the Army, often away, so there was no one around to notice whether I ate or not. My self-loathing had grown alongside a huge, cold stone in my stomach that left no room for anything else.

Years passed. My identity was wrapped up in making myself useful and helping others. I tried to find my significance through theirs. I volunteered for worthy organizations and causes. And I didn't just volunteer. I was the Chair, President, or whatever the Chick-in-Charge was called on virtually everything I put my hand to. My need to be significant required constant feeding. So, I kept building my tower high in the sky, far from who I felt was always lurking below. *Insignificant me. Unworthy me.* That was the real me, wasn't it? The "less than" me. I needed to escape her.

Eventually, I weighed only 84 pounds, and my best friend Carla, a nurse, confronted me. She put a name to my behavior. Anorexia. I was embarrassed and furious with her for calling it out. With her patience and some convincing, I checked myself into an eating disorder hospital back in Kentucky. Her firm, loving willingness to walk with me into raw transparency was the first step on my journey to healing.

At that time, I healed part of my mind from the eating disorder that attempted to make my body disappear. But I didn't wholly stand up to the inner menace that held me hostage for another twenty-five-plus years. All the therapy, counseling, self-analysis, medications, and holistic practices only moved me so far toward my goal of embracing the "real me." To be honest, I didn't know what the phrase "the real me" even meant. I always seemed to miss the mark in most areas of my life. Nothing was ever good enough. *I was never good enough.* This was a house of cards built on lies. And it all came crashing down.

The only way to build my identity anew was to start at the foundation where my authentic voice was waiting for me all along. I found it indirectly through the greatest literary voice of all time, William Shakespeare. Some of the most common expressions we use every day are plucked from the lines of his works penned over 420 years ago. Have you ever "been in a pickle" that led you on "a wild goose chase" because the "green-eyed monster" convinced you that you'd "seen better days" because after all "love is blind" so "good riddance"? Yep. Shakespeare.

Here's my connection to The Bard: I discovered, as part of my search for the real MaryAnn, that I enjoy stage acting. Especially performing Shakespeare. In one of his masterpieces, *Macbeth*, the Scottish Lord opines about all the tomorrows in one's life as a mortal man, "...struts and frets his hour upon the stage and then is heard no more." Granted, things were bleak as he'd just received word that Lady Macbeth was dead, but there's wisdom in his words for you and me in the 21st century.

At least one thing hasn't changed in the whole span of human existence. And I'm not being dramatic when I say: *You have a finite amount of time.* What are you waiting for? A soul-piercing shriek? Please don't wait, my fine, courageous friend. Your inner critic won't stop lying to you about who you really are until you learn the truth. Chapter 3 shows you how to do just that by accessing your unique strengths, free of the inner critic's distortions, revealing your authentic self and your courageous howl.

Now it's your turn to begin to unleash authentic you with some practical application.

Meet me at Pause & Practice for Chapter 2 in the back of the book.

3

SEEING YOUR STRENGTHS CLEARLY

Through the Looking Glass

Do you wear eyeglasses or know someone who does? People who need glasses often recall receiving their first pair of glasses and seeing clearly for the first time. Objects look crisper, colors sharper, and the world brighter. When I first got readers, I was amazed at how farsightedness was affecting my ability to see anything clearly. Even my plate of food; eating had become unappetizing because the plate was blurry. Then this realization set in: before glasses, I saw the world around me unclearly. Making one simple adjustment completely changed my view of reality to one of greater clarity.

Clarity is an often misunderstood concept. Webster's dictionary defines clarity as "the quality or state of being clear." We tend to assume that means we speak and write to others "clearly"—in a manner that conveys exactly what we're thinking, so they'll understand. We need to be clear and specific, so we aren't misunderstood. Or we think of clarity as a way of valuing gemstones; the more expensive diamond has greater clarity. While those concepts aren't wrong, those superficial understandings of clarity can separate us from its most important, amazing quality.

The greatest clarity must always begin with self. If we're not crystal clear within ourselves, the only outcome is that we cause those around us to misunderstand who we are, what we intend to express, and our values. Much like Alice's experience in the famous Lewis Carroll story, things can seem quite distorted when outside influences obscure our inner view. Our world doesn't make sense. We may wonder: *How did I wind up here? I don't want to be here.*

The clarity of seeing yourself through the lens of your innate strengths is like putting on glasses for the first time; your whole world changes. Yes, your *whole world.* Once you discover your natural strengths, your authentic superpower comes into focus. You see the brighter and sharper you, and you won't be able to unsee its majesty. At first, this exciting, somehow familiar, and simultaneously somewhat unfamiliar view of yourself can take some getting used to. But it's ah-mazing.

Now, you may be thinking, "Whoa, MaryAnn, that's a bit high-minded, isn't it?" Nope, and here's why: When we deny our innate self-knowledge, we unwittingly embolden our inner critic. We can have a proclivity to look outside ourselves for the truth, needlessly complicating our identity and self-worth, which causes confusion. Here are some tactics your inner critic may have tried on you:

- Comparison– leading to instant unhappiness.
- Fixation on Failure– keeping you locked in fear mode afraid to try anything.
- Fear of Mistakes– obsessing over every detail or "what if" that can balloon into overworking and burnout.
- Amnesia– proving yourself over and over, forgetting past successes.
- Unreasonable Expectations– painting false pictures of the perfect "how it's supposed to be" so your results never seem like enough.

Each of those pitfalls can lead to exhaustion and disillusionment because we resort to old thought patterns and habits instead of using our superpowers. We muzzle our Towanda.

The inner critic will hijack your unique and authentic voice, siphoning your might. I lived that way for years. Patsy (aka my inner critic-you'll hear more about her later) caused me to doubt everything I knew deep

Thomas Edison said, "If we all did the things we are capable of doing, we would literally astound ourselves."

down to be true about myself. That was before I tuned into my superpowers, my strengths, and how reliable they are. I 100% could trust them. Finally, I understood what American inventor, Thomas Edison, meant when he said, "If we all did the things we are capable of doing, we would literally astound ourselves." (How poetic that these words were spoken by a man whose invention of the light bulb brings clarity to the darkness).

Stronger Than I Know

In my search for guidance, I read self-help books and tried tools like meditation and gratitude, which helped me make progress. Nothing seemed wholly adequate for the gnarled threads of my life. Then I remembered an assessment I completed years earlier while serving as a nonprofit executive—the Gallup® CliftonStrengths® assessment. It was founded by psychologist, academic researcher, and former Gallup®, Inc. Chairman, Dr. Don Clifton. He and his research team identified thirty-four core talent themes grouped from a larger pool of traits. Some talents bear names like Activator®, Command®, Intellection®, Futuristic®, and Maximizer®, etc.

The assessment matches each person with their talents by asking a series of questions about preferences, tendencies, and values. The assessment is so granular, the odds of you and another person having the exact same order of just the Top 5 themes is... one in 33 million. I was astounded by the accuracy of my assessment, but not exactly thrilled with my Top 5 results: Input®, Intellection®, Learner®, Activator®, and Responsibility®. *Yawn. What a snore fest.* Except for Activator®, I didn't consider them very–dynamic. I wanted talents like Command® or Maximizer®.

But as I learned the specifics of my strengths, I realized just how much they made sense and leaned into them. My Input®, Intellection®, and Learner® ensured that I brought accurate information my team needed for projects; my Activator® took leadership action so the projects moved forward; and my Responsibility® made sure that I did what I said I would—with excellence. Gallup® research shows that people who put their strengths into practice every day are six times more likely to be engaged at work and 8% more productive than their counterparts. I realized significant results in both markers.

As I navigated the twists and turns of my struggles with refreshed self-awareness, I felt a loosening of the muzzle my inner critic used to silence me. A path emerged, leading back to authentic me—the one-of-a-kind fearfully, wonderfully, and specially designed *me* I'd been created to be.

My connection with authentic me grew stronger, and my communication with my Creator became more organic. It was real and personal, like a conversation with the best friend I'd ever known. I found the courage to trust that 1:1 relationship. My faith in Christ was healthier than it had ever been. Mother Father God became real to me again. I'd returned to a simple faith of innocence. Uncomplicated. Close. Curious. Unobscured.

During the first few years of living into my new healthy howl, I felt like a wolf pup expressing its first *aaa-ooos*. Not as mighty as they'd eventually become, but enthusiastic, nonetheless. I grew in self-actualization. I learned that the still small whisper is our knowing of truth, calling into question the status quo to which we've become accustomed. The howl is our fearless, Authentic

You, fed up with being bullied by our condescending inner critic, crying out for us to rise. When those whispers are dismissed or ignored, sometimes, as was my experience, the authentic self escalates into a painful shriek to wake us out of complacency.

In the aftermath of my Towanda blaze of glory, I felt a conviction to share the benefits of my lived experience and the wisdom it had brought, helping people like you discover, embrace, and step into their full, unique potential. As the executive director of a nonprofit leadership development organization, I began speaking at women's events, leading workshops, conducting seminars, and mentoring others. Yet my spirit remained restless. Dozens of possibilities of "what could be" skipped around inside my head. I was being called into a season of higher purpose for myself and my fellow travelers. My soul was stirring. Its whisper in my ear hinted at the howl that was building in my heart.

The time arrived for me to step away from my job and take the plunge. I invested in myself, becoming a full-time, hang-up-my-own-shingle entrepreneur, a Certified Gallup® Strengths Coach. I'd taken all of the personality tests you can think of, but none of them were as granular, practical, and actionable as my experience with Gallup® CliftonStrengths®. I knew it would be an important part of my authentic life path. No surprise, my inner critic took this decision as her marching orders, too, just in a different direction. But I was onto her modus operandi by then, so I kept my gaze upward and pushed even harder into my strengths.

I climbed higher, fueled by the assurance and peace that came from aligning with my inner Towanda. I would live my life with fearless authenticity—no regrets about whispers and howls that went unheeded. Just wolf pups know they can take on the world, I was ready.

CliftonStrengths® is an amazing tool that helped change my life. Today, I incorporate it with clients on the journey to their version of genuine success and a fulfilled life. The inner critic hates that because knowing your strengths gives you one of the greatest weapons in your arsenal–raw clarity of self.

Your Strengths Matter

When you bring the best of authentic you center stage, your inner critic doesn't stand a chance. Is there an area where your inner critic has a stronghold? If so, the key to amplifying your authentic voice is to apply your strengths in everyday life. By strengths, I mean your talent DNA, as defined by Don Clifton, dubbed by the American Psychological Association as the "father of strengths-based psychology." He writes in *Strengths 2.0* that, "A strength is the ability to consistently produce a positive outcome through near-perfect performance in a specific task." You can discover your Top 5 strengths through the CliftonStrengths® Assessment. The link is located in the introduction and at the back of this book. Clifton's assessment measures your natural talents and provides resources and effective ways you can amplify those talents into strengths.

When you bring the best of authentic you center stage, your inner critic doesn't stand a chance.

In Clifton's model, a 'talent' is defined as "… a naturally recurring pattern of thought, feeling, or behavior that can be productively applied." As we learn how this potential shows up to support the best version of us, we can intentionally apply our talents each day. With consistent practice, they mature into reliable strengths and guide us toward how we're hard-wired to excel. Conversely, they can also show us how we won't experience our highest and best. Try and try as you might, it'll be like forcing a square peg into a round hole.

More than the generalities of personality tests that can help determine *where you might succeed*, CliftonStrengths® identifies your natural talent, showing you *how you will succeed*. Engaging from a place of natural strength, you can express your authentic voice and pursue your goals and dreams with reliable confidence. This clarity is a powerful foe of the inner critic.

The data on the impact of CliftonStrengths® is irrefutable. As of the printing of this book, over 34 million people have taken the CS Assessment across 247 countries. To analyze employee productivity, Gallup's scientists formally measure engagement, along with "active disengagement." That term is often bandied about by frustrated human resource professionals attempting to improve the workplace. Clifton defines active disengagement as "… a state where an employee is not only unhappy with their job but actively expresses their discontent by undermining their colleagues, complaining frequently, and generally behaving in a negative manner."

After measuring both employee engagement and active disengagement, the scientists identified some compelling statistics. Here are a few:

- People who focus on their strengths are three times likely to report having an excellent quality of life.
- People who use their strengths every day are six times more likely to be engaged on the job.
- People who use their strengths every day have 7.8% greater productivity.
- Managers who focus on employees' strengths reduce active disengagement to an astonishingly low 1%.

The positive applications of leaning into our strengths, personally and professionally, are more than impressive. They can transform individual lives and bring a workplace culture from dreaded to desired.

Getting Personal with Your Strengths

Your strengths are the true North of your life's compass, offering guidance toward better choices, taking decisive action, and remaining accountable to your purpose. When I'm speaking to audiences and utter the word 'purpose,' people can go into a panic, thinking they must discover the *one* reason God put them on this Earth. I spent a good deal of my life on a quest for certainty of my *one* purpose. I'm glad those days are behind me. Your purpose will look different in different seasons of life.

Living a strengths-based life simplifies the process because cultivating self-acceptance and embracing your uniqueness builds stability. Otherwise, you're building on top of a sinkhole, instead of good, solid limestone like the kind the water here flows through bringing life to our fine Kentucky bourbon. Your unique strengths provide a firm foundation keeping you sure-footed versus trying to keep your balance when the ground beneath you feels unstable. Things around you may collapse but not you. You're on solid ground and confident in who you are.

Where before your inner critic kept you spinning in indecision and doubt, high-level self-leadership becomes your norm.

Embracing your strengths unlocks your power to create the environment you want.

Authentic You develops 20/20 vision, a clearer understanding of why you're better at some things than others, and that it's perfectly okay. It reduces self-judgment. Others have their strengths. You have your strengths. The differences don't have to mean envy, unhealthy competition, or in the extreme—paranoia.

Embracing your strengths unlocks your power to create the environment you want, guilt-free, without trying to please or impress others. This was a large part of my journey. As a public speaker and stage actress, people can assume that I want to be out front, that I need to be. Actually, my strengths present a different story. One that I ran up against for a lot of my life.

Among my top strengths are Intellection® and Focus®, which thrive with time alone. A lot of time passed before I realized those strengths are why I felt so drained after multiple speaking engagements. Others can go, go, go day after day, but I need time to reenergize. I love speaking and sharing with groups, and being on stage with fellow thespians is exhilarating, but I must have downtime. So, I created a serene environment where I can reflect, contemplate, opine, journal, consider, read, and ruminate. I've learned how that act of self-care is necessary to honor my mental, emotional, spiritual, and physical wellness.

My Responsibility® strength thrives when I remember that my first responsibility is to my authenticity and what nourishes it. Living in the guidance of my strengths keeps me on track, and when I veer off course and I respect them, they easily bring me back to balance. When I'm out of alignment with my talents, I can become on edge, overwhelmed, irritable, claustrophobic, and without fail will fall to some 'unexpected' illness, which now I know should be totally expected.

When you respect those healthy boundaries, you have an advantage over your inner critic because it no longer controls the expression of self, you do. You can invest in people and projects without feeling depleted because your essential building blocks are being met, energizing you to bring your A-game to what matters for this season of life.

A clear, strengths-based vision is attended by fearlessness. I don't mean to imply you'll never be afraid, but you will fear less. You'll begin to notice things that previously caused your inner critic to activate are happening less. When you're guided by the strength of your authenticity, there's innate confidence present. You don't have to pretend. There's no imposter syndrome.

Your "knowing" is visceral. Instead of sinking, you soar. You'll find yourself "in the zone" or "in the flow" because you're showing up and doing what you do best every day. Your confidence grows— aaaa-woooo!—even more, and challenges become opportunities to shine. I'm reminded of this as I sit here writing by my son's pool. I just looked up, and two hours have passed in what felt like thirty minutes. Where my inner critic once had me agonizing for hours saying, "You'll never write a book," just now, fearless authenticity howled, "*Aaaaa-ooooo!* On to the next page!"

Katie's Story

My client, Katie, a successful local tourism director, felt a restless stirring to do more. She didn't know it yet, but her authentic self was whispering to her about new ways to serve. Yet, Katie had a young family and enjoyed the flexibility of working in her hometown. While that "should" have been enough for her, the stirring remained. Exasperated, she asked, "Do I stay, or do I go?"

One day her exciting-and-terrifying-all-at-the-same-time answer came. She heard about an opening for the Vice-President of the Kentucky Derby Museum. Katie and I both live in the "all things horse" part of Kentucky and if you've ever watched the most exciting two minutes in sports, you know that we take our horses seriously—very seriously. She was immediately interested. And it didn't take long for her inner critic to be off to the races with negative thoughts pounding her mind like horses' hooves.

She told me all about it during a coaching session. "MaryAnn, you wouldn't believe how vicious my inner critic is," she sighed.

I grabbed a pen. "Tell me."

"Here goes," and she began listing the negative thoughts, counting them on her fingers from one to five. I wrote them all down:

1. You're too young for this high-level position.
2. No one's going to take you seriously.
3. If you make a mistake, everyone will know—it's the Kentucky Derby, for Christ's sake!
4. Will you abandon your team and department here you worked so hard to build?
5. You won't have time for your kids if you make this move.

Sound familiar?

I reminded her that she was a *leading expert* on harnessing tourism's positive economic impact, while remaining loyal to the history, culture, and values held by generational residents of a community. She'd accomplished much in her career, had built a dynamic team, nurtured fruitful partnerships, led a statewide industry association, and was highly regarded across the region and beyond for her leadership in the tourism sector. I asked, "Does that sound like the resume of a newbie no one would listen to?"

"Not really," she said. I had her look at her strengths again. We discussed the value she naturally brings to the world and what she needs to feel energized and genuinely fulfilled. "Maybe I do have everything I need inside to take the leap," she admitted.

By harnessing (pardon the pun) those natural strengths and using them to propel herself into a life of success—on her terms—she possessed all the confidence she needed to quiet the negative voices. But I couldn't believe it for her. She had to own the power and edge her strengths afforded her. One of Katie's top strengths is focus. We decided to direct her focus toward clarifying what she really wanted, how to sustain it, and ensuring it aligned with her values.

"The bottom line is one question," I said. "Will this career move help you realize the life you want for yourself and your family?"

She flashed me a confident smile. "I already knew the answer. I think I just needed a reminder that I have everything I need to get there," she said.

She applied for the position and got it. Since she's been promoted to Executive Vice President of the iconic brand. Katie says living in her strengths gives her confidence to make big, bold decisions for her future. Every day she champions her staff to do what they do best at work and in their home life for the ones *they* love.

You're no different than Katie. She has her superpowers. You have yours. They're your natural talents when applied intentionally become trusted strengths. They're just waiting for you to rely on them as your unique power and edge.

Do you hear those whispers? Are they getting louder? *Yep.* That's the desire to climb to the top of your mountain and howl from your fearless authentic voice that you're ready to show up and serve.

When Your Inner Critic Zig Zags

While your strengths are the high performing expression of your talents in balance, never forget that your inner critic is a master manipulator. One of its trickier strategies is zigzagging. Zig—one of your strengths (or more than one) is being over-expressed; or Zag—it's being under-expressed. The inner critic twists them into their rawest, unpolished forms.

Let's take Achiever® as an example. Gallup's definition for this talent theme states: "People exceptionally talented in the Achiever® theme work hard and possess a great deal of stamina. They take immense satisfaction in being busy and productive." Sounds great, huh? It is when in balance. When the inner critic zigs you into over-expressing your Achiever®, you may have a jam-packed calendar because you're overcommitted with no margin in your days, which turn into weeks, then years. Your inner critic sets you up with a lifestyle of needing to "do" more and more. In his book, *Margin*, author Richard Swenson uses the analogy of the white space on a page of notebook paper. There are boundary lines. Look at the page you're reading. Writing doesn't fill up the entire page. Achiever® that is over-expressed fills up all of your space and time until there's no white space left. No margin.

Achiever is #7 out of my Top 10 strengths. I understand this "fill all the time" manipulation by the inner critic. Having a margin in my life used to scare me. I was convinced that "idle" time meant I was unproductive and not proving my value. I was critical of others I perceived as not productive enough. They were lazy and entitled. Sure, they could goof off. The rest of us were carrying the load to keep society moving forward. *Sheesh.* What a relief it was when I took myself off that merry-go-round. A balanced Achiever® keeps me a much happier and more satisfied gal.

What about Achiever® as under-expressed? Then, you have lost sight of your 'why.' Sure, you work hard and have great stamina to stay productive, but at what cost? A human cost. The 'work' itself becomes the most important thing. Completing it drives you. You may find yourself unable to leave work at work, never able to turn it off. Others who set boundaries between work and family may actually irritate you. Your inner critic causes you to view them through a negative lens.

On the surface, prioritizing work over all else sounds almost admirable. The inner critic loves that zag because it can create tunnel vision in which you lose sight of the consequences; the impact on your health, your friends, and your family. Overworking reduces you to merely a tool doing a job—period. Either extreme of the spectrum brings you out of alignment with the strength of your authenticity, which satisfies the inner critic's goal. Being out of balance with your strengths leaves you out of alignment with your highest and best authentic self, and instead, you align with the inner critic.

When you observe yourself, notice that imbalance, and acknowledge the implications, you'll hear the whisper of an untapped strength yearning to exist in its optimal state—authentic, powerful, balanced. Then, it elevates your well-being and that of those around you, a true strength. (And trust me, this is the last thing your inner critic wants you to know).

Now you've learned the secret of discovering your superpowers. You've had this power inside you all along; you just needed to unleash your authentic self. The best home you'll ever know is to live confidently and authentically in your skin. And that's great news for the rest of us. We need you.

Turn to the back of this book for instructions for taking the CliftonStrengths® assessment. Discover your strengths to build your arsenal before meeting your inner critic and going toe-to-toe in Chapter 4. To continue on your trajectory of building self-knowing and clarity there are resources waiting for you.

Meet me at Pause & Practice for Chapter 3 in the back of the book.

4

KNOW THY ENEMY

Internal Combat

Since your earliest memories, your inner critic has sown doubts, leading you to distrust yourself and ignore who you were created to be—brilliant and complete. As you learned in Chapter 2, your unique talents were vanquished and held captive long before you could fully experience your joyful howl. The inner critic seeks to scare you into believing the only way to be safe is to deny yourself and muzzle your amazing, vibrant spirit. Now that you're armed with your unique strengths from Chapter 3, you're prepared for internal combat.

Essentially, your inner critic is a homegrown terrorist that has infiltrated your mind. Your mind is a battleground that you must reclaim in the name of your authentic self. If that sounds melodramatic, it's not. *This is war.* And you must win each battle along the way in the fight for your freedom.

To wage proper combat, start by acknowledging the enemy's assault-style tactics. The inner critic slithers deep in the shadows and learns your patterns and behaviors, becoming an expert on what makes you tick, especially the gaps and weaknesses. This sleeper agent lurks until the perfect opportunity when you're vulnerable; then, it shoots down the first murmur of self-truth with the precision of a sniper. But when you know what signs to look for, you can pre-empt the inner critic and neutralize the threat.

Meeting Your Inner Critic

We often mistake the inner critic for a "good angel" or our conscience, looking out for and protecting us from bad decisions. An inner voice was simply guiding me to a better way, so ignoring it could lead to peril. Then I learned better. Make no mistake: *The inner critic doesn't have your best interests at heart.* I didn't realize that every time I acquiesced, every time I gave in to the negative voice, and every time I agreed there was a new fault to be found; little by little, I was losing the ability to trust myself.

When you know what signs to look for, you can pre-empt the inner critic and neutralize the threat.

Before living a strengths-based life, I was complicit in making everything Patsy whispered in my ear my truth. I agreed that she was right. I wasn't good enough. I was wrong. I couldn't trust myself. "Who's Patsy," you ask? It's time for intros.

Patsy is my inner critic. She's been with me a long time. Believe it or not, my inner critic is an eight-year-old girl with long pigtails. I apologize upfront to all the nice "Patsys" in the world. Don't email, post on social media, write to my publisher, or otherwise share that you're offended. Sorry. I'm sure you're lovely. My Patsy was anything but nice.

In the beginning, I thought she was so pretty and poised. She was in the other third-grade class, and we rode the same school bus. She always wound up sitting next to me. She had the nicest store-bought clothes. Mine were homemade. She had pretty, colored satin ribbons tied at the ends of her long, perfect pigtails. My hair hung down the length of my back straight and was pulled back with a single brown barrette. She had beautiful fingernails, too. Perfectly shaped just over the ends of her fingers. I bit mine down to the quick. My mother put a bitter solution on my fingers, hoping I'd stop. Every few minutes, my tongue got a stinging reminder that I was failing…again.

Sometimes, Patsy would reach over and dig her perfect fingernails into my arm as she whispered, "You're so skinny and ugly. No wonder everyone calls you 'toothpick.'" She was right. I was skinny and wasn't as pretty as the other girls. I had a broken front tooth from the local dentist's son tripping me the year before during a game of Duck, Duck, Goose, causing me to faceplant on the hard gymnasium floor.

I dreaded seeing the big, yellow bus coming to a stop at Patsy's house. My stomach would become a knot of anxiety. Still, I wanted her to like me. So, I'd tell her how pretty her dress was or how much I liked her ruffled socks. I pretended it didn't hurt when she scratched my arm.

My mother noticed the scratches one day, and I blamed them on my cat, Smokey. When there were new ones the next day, my mother probed a bit deeper. I came clean about Patsy. She stopped stirring the pot that was on the stove. I almost thought she was going to pull me to her and console me. Instead, she said, "I can't believe you're letting some silly young'un do that to you. You tell her to stop. If you come home with scratches one more time, you'll get a spanking."

I began avoiding Patsy. Some days it worked. Other days, she'd wait for me to get off the school bus and whisper something mean. Then something glorious happened. Patsy's family moved. But since I never stood up to her, she didn't really go away. The external pain stopped. The internal hurts remained. My experience with Patsy was a symptom of all the ways my inner critic had already hijacked my self-worth.

We all hear our inner critic mocking us, but few are willing to grab her by those greasy pigtails and toss her off the anxiety playground she's making of your mind. We'd rather ignore the faultfinder inside our head, hoping it will just go away, than face it. That never works. It can't go *poof*, as much as we wish it would. Pretending the inner critic isn't there or doesn't affect us is a lie that doesn't stop the destruction. The longer we allow it to hold a power position in our lives, the deeper we fall into its trap of limiting beliefs.

So, if you've ever wondered, "Isn't there some way to shut her up?"

There is.

Going Into Battle

While I healed a part of my mind from the eating disorder that had attempted to make my body disappear, I remained comfortable with my inner critic forbidding my authentic self to speak. A lot more time passed before I wholly stood up to the familiar menace inside that held me hostage. I couldn't have predicted the chain of events that would push me to the precipice of making the scariest and most liberating decision of my life—choosing to discover who I really was at the core level and accepting it as good. Not simply good but *designed, intentional,* and *wonderful.*

I told you in Chapter 1 about the day a painful howl forced me to stop ignoring my true heart, soul, and mind. I drew that line in the sand and said, "Enough."

I was forty-six years old, and my life's pattern was to live in lockdown control mode, keeping tight parameters on everything. I'd always tried to do everything right. Kept *all* the rules—of my parents, society, and religion. Did what was expected of me. Did what I was told. Did what others thought was best for me. I lived day in and day out with a familiar routine of dismissing my thoughts, wishes, and needs. Don't mess up. Don't let your kids mess up and embarrass you or the family. Be the perfect daughter. Be the perfect Army wife. Be the perfect mother. My charge was simple, right? Just be... *perfect.* Just that one thing. If others saw me that way, then it would be true. One day, I'd be good enough. Then I'd find my value and worth.

I ignored the yearnings of my authentic voice. It was reduced to that laryngitic whisper while Patsy was howling louder than ever. And yet that almost imperceptible whisper kept calling to me in the same mantra, "Trust Me. When you trust Me, I can help you find the courage to trust yourself."

I ignored the yearnings of my authentic voice.

For some reason that I still don't quite understand, the situation with my teenage daughter's stroke and learning of her boyfriend's abuse was my breaking point. I kept replaying how I could've prevented it over in my head. How her boyfriend's cruelty was somehow my fault. Of course, that was nonsense, but I'd thought that way my entire life.

I surely did everything right when they started dating. I thought I had everything under control. I asked questions, met the parents, was inside their house, and still, my precious daughter had been wounded. *The truth was painfully clear.* Perfection and Control were myths. Everything my inner critic had been howling in my ear was a Big Fat Lie.

None of the controlling, rule-keeping, coloring inside the lines perfectionism had kept what lurks in the shadows from hurting me; and now it was hurting my child. Deep down, I knew that my strict approach to life had likely been detrimental to my children in some ways. It certainly hadn't been healthy for me growing up. It would be painful to clean the wounds.

The hurts of my heart, soul, mind, and body felt like an animal with its leg caught in a trap. Only I was the animal, and it was my voice being cut off. And I was fed up. In deciding enough was enough, I gathered the courage to trust myself and took the first and most critical step of the journey—stepping onto the battlefield to face my inner critic head-on. It would be a *fight*. But Patsy had been calling the shots long enough.

I went toe-to-toe with my inner critic. My very primal **"Enough!"** carried a lifetime of muzzled grief. My whisper became a full-on howl, refusing to be ignored for one more second. This howl wasn't a squall of retreating in pain. It was a war cry compelling me to triumph. The howl demanded my full attention. It deserved my full attention. The remainder of my time on earth deserved unwavering devotion to my highest authentic self.

Noël's Story

My client, Noël, has a story that highlights what it looks like to listen to the whisper inside your heart and unleash it, to take your business to a next level howl. She was already a highly successful independent marketing executive and wellness educator. But at times, she found having sales conversations with potential clients a daunting task. Her heart-centered leadership style made connecting with people in genuinely caring ways of paramount importance to her. Her goals in business and life centered on serving people and bringing lasting positive change to their health and well-being. Since she worked for herself, she was responsible for cultivating many of her business leads.

We met at a women's retreat in Kentucky at Snug Hollow Farm, in the same cabin, actually, where Jojo Moyes wrote *The Giver of Stars*. When you're sharing sleeping quarters with someone, you get to know them pretty quickly.

I spotted Noël's natural strengths and how they'd supported her in her life as I learned more about her:

–She's a previously divorced mother of 2 girls.
–She spent many years as a single mother.
–She has a military family and is very patriotic.

  –And she's passionate about turning hopelessness into hopefulness.

Deep down, though, she knew she wasn't using her strengths to their fullest potential. There was more out there for her. She could feel it. But something was holding her back.

We stayed in touch after the retreat. Eventually, I became a customer of hers (I'm always looking for ways to make my home and body healthier), and she became a coaching client.

Noël had taken the Gallup® CliftonStrengths assessment eight years before we worked together. It's no surprise that Noël has Positivity®, Maximizer®, and Relator® in her Top 5 strengths. She was fascinated by how accurate her results still were. "I guess some things just never change," she laughed. "I was created to be this way, so let's make the most of it!"

We took a hard look at her inner critic's tactics and strategized how she could combine her various strengths. She wanted to apply them to a variety of situations to transform her professional and personal life. We also identified a more authentic way she could communicate with new leads, so she could really connect with them and grow her business: "My strengths enable me to come in with a message that really resonates with each individual. I look at my strengths every day and I ask, 'How can I best use these strengths today to help people?'"

Because of Noël's renewed commitment to self, she's noticed improvement in several areas of her business, including:

- Learning how & when to combine her innate strengths.
- Approaching new leads in a manner best suited to them.
- Understanding & inspiring her team better.
- Taking control of her inner critic.

Noël's learned to blend her strengths in a range of scenarios; "It's interesting to see how the different combinations of strengths can play into supporting my business." This most often shows up when Noël is speaking with potential customers. Now, she easily recognized others' strengths and navigated conversations with confidence.

Neutralize the Threat

On my journey to discover, acknowledge, and embrace the fearless, unapologetic, authentic me, I had to bring to light the many things that previously prevented me from liberating myself from negativity. You read about these earlier: I was an adopted kid with abandonment issues, I had suffered childhood sexual trauma, I coped with a near fatal bout with anorexia nervosa, and my inner critic had kept me on a wild pendulum ride with perfectionism and judgment at one extreme and anxiety and depression at the other.

Whatever heartbreak has seemed to define your past, you're strong enough to meet your inner critic—up close and personal. *I know, I know.* That root canal you've been putting off isn't looking so bad right now. I hear you. "*No,* thanks, MaryAnn! Are you nuts? Dig *deeper* into all the things that make me feel 'less than' and that scream 'you suck!'?"

Haven't you let your Patsy run around in your head making trouble long enough? Don't worry. We're in this together. And here's a secret: *You're brave enough to do hard things.* Remember that "thing" you never thought you could endure. Made it through that, didn't ya? Of course, you did, and you can do this. Put those shoulders back and let's meet your inner critic face to face because you're about to go toe to toe.

Mine shows up in her greasy pigtails and snotty nose, trying to take me back to times when I felt my weakest, most embarrassed, and pathetic. Like the time in the fourth grade when Ethan Johnson nailed me in the face with a dodgeball during recess, and everyone laughed their heads off when I hit the ground. Horrific and demoralizing then. Now, not so much.

To neutralize your inner critic, you must pre-empt the strikes and take her or him out first. This requires a "recon," background research on the enemy. Take some time to think through the events in your life when your inner critic originated. Notice the inner voice you heard. What did it say? How did it make you feel? What did you do to try and quiet it? Maybe sometimes you heard and heeded your authentic voice. And other times, what you thought was your "good angel" keeping you out of harm may have been your inner critic discounting your truth.

Remember, your inner critic is the voice that demeans you. It magnifies every perceived "flaw," blurring the clarity of your authentic self. The inner critic is an expert at morphing into just the right little (or gigantic) monster depending on how you're feeling physically, emotionally, mentally, or spiritually at the time. It burrows into your mind like an earworm, except instead of songs like "Baby Shark" or "Umbrella," you'll hear your classic self-criticism tracks. In fact, I even made a list of The Inner Critic's Top Ten Hits:

- Insists that you're inherently flawed. If you've suffered early trauma, it'll try to convince you there is no way to overcome having been a victim.
- Convinces you that your wants, things that please you, are either inherently wrong or not as important as others' desires.
- Says you don't fit in and keeps you on edge, repeating negative statements others important to you have said about you; worries that you'll be judged and not fully accepted by others.
- Uses a hypercritical lens to magnify perceived imperfections and demands you to be perfect.

Q Set standards so high you have difficulty completing tasks because you feel no matter how hard you work or how successful—it's never enough.

Q Is severe with you and can shame you in certain situations, attacking your self-worth with precision.

Q Keeps you adhering to standards set by others, religion, community, and culture. You're safe from rejection if people in those circles admire and like you. Exclusion surely awaits if you believe, think, or feel differently.

Q Makes you believe that you're mediocre or even worse, lazy, and failure could be just around the corner.

Q Wants you to live in guilt, unable to forgive yourself for wrongs you have committed against yourself or others.

Q Keeps you from striving beyond your comfort zone. Risk taking is often a big no-no because you could be judged, hurt, or worst of all—rejected. The only way to protect yourself is to never forget your mistakes or try again.

Additionally, within those characterizations of the inner critic, there are four archetypes your inner critic uses to its advantage. To further strengthen your arsenal take the What's Your Inner Critic's Personality Type quiz: www.calmyourinnercritic.com/quiz to identify which archetype your inner critic shows up as and what works best to subdue it. (You'll also find the quiz link in this chapter's Pause & Practice). You neutralize the threat by knowing and calming the inner critic, disarming it of its power over your authentic self. Before moving on to Chapter 5, where you'll learn how to channel this newfound freedom into fearless authenticity, take some time to work the exercises to help support you during this phase.

Meet me at Pause & Practice for Chapter 4 in the back of the book.

5

EMBRACING
AUTHENTIC YOU

Many of us travel through life often disconnected from our deeper feelings. In a variety of ways, we numb unpleasant emotions and spend our time presenting the socially acceptable side of ourselves. As I championed my authentic self, the nature of my inner battle shifted. I began accessing the freedom I was fighting for—to howl my inner truth. In doing so, I peeled back the layers of my inner critic's deception and saw what I was made of. Our mind has us convinced that if we traverse beyond the inner critic's warnings, a stinging darkness awaits us. Like slicing open an onion, the closer our blade cuts toward the core, the more painful the reveal.

In my process, I uncovered truths that were unexpected—and at times, unsettling. But, by giving them a voice, even those that scared me, I saw their intended use and embraced them. This can happen for you, too. We achieve fearless authenticity when unlocking the howl feels safer than keeping it under lock and key. And by breaking out of our inner-critic-inspired holding patterns, we bring the full force of our strengths to our life's purpose.

An Untried Design

Both of my grandmothers were quilters. I remember watching them at their hoops. I'm fortunate to have some of their beautiful handiwork and even a few creations by my great-grandmother. Perhaps because of this influence, I often think about how life is much like a quilt. It isn't created overnight or in one sitting. Finishing a single coverlet can take weeks. The same is true of stitching your authentic self together over time, choosing courage and truth over fear and silence, piece by piece.

For most of my life, I focused on my quilt's top layer—the star of the show—the face. The attention I received from others seemed to always be on outward aesthetics. How I appeared to those around me. Was I acceptable to them in how I looked, spoke, my ideas, and my abilities? When I didn't measure up, which felt like most of the time, I'd try to make myself more appealing by copying others' patterns of stitches to put myself together in a way others would accept. But my focus was misplaced.

The real star of the most beautiful quilts isn't what appears on the surface but in the stitches running through the entire quilt from the top layer through the batting into the back layer. You see, quilts have five components:

1. The back, where everything else attaches and provides the foundation.
2. The batting that fills the middle for warmth.
3. The top or face where the quilter's design is featured.
4. The stitches or "quilting" that hold it all together.
5. The binding that encloses the rough edges of the fabric to prevent it from coming apart.

So, the quilting is the most important component of the quilt. Without it, the quilt will unravel without serving its purpose to provide love, warmth, comfort, and a sense of security for someone.

When I finally said "enough" to my inner critic at the age of forty-seven, I knew my stitching and binding needed repair. My life's quilt hadn't been properly cared for and was of little use to me or anyone else, especially my teenage daughter, who needed me. The quality of the thread was poor, so the original stitching had come loose, allowing the binding to slip from the quilt top. The fabric was exposed and frayed. Things were holding together as best as they could with my minimal attention—some cheap seam tape here and a little fabric glue there. But when put under more stressful conditions, the quilt began falling apart. Temporary fixes weren't the answer. Patching the threadbare places wasn't enough.

The design components of my life's quilt needed a thorough examination, layer by layer and stitch by stitch. I'd save the best parts and let the rest go. Certain habits and fears had served their lifespan and needed to be relegated to the scrap bin. But letting go of what's familiar isn't easy. Familiar is known. Untried can be scary.

Even though a pattern in your life is no longer serving you and really wasn't made with the best materials to begin with, it may feel familiar like an old, worn, threadbare quilt. You may wonder, "If I let go of the old, familiar pieces of myself, will I still have the love, warmth, comfort, and security I need?" The inner critic's whispers of fear and scarcity can leave you feeling trapped and resigned that the 'something more' your authentic voice is calling you to isn't going to be all you've hoped for. That's another big, fat lie.

You have the strength to answer your inner critic's warnings with your fearless, authentic voice howling a resounding *yes*. Yes, you'll have the good things you want in life, and the work you're doing here and now, now to calm your inner critic makes you ready to receive them. Instead of your inner critic restricting you, you can teach her to trust Authentic You to lead the way toward expansion.

Today, I know the real me that I thought I'd never find, and I love her. (I'm pretty amazing. And here's a secret—you're *amazing*, too). You have God-given, authentic strengths, and you can use them to quilt any pattern to fulfill any purpose you desire.

Your Authentic Voice

The most natural way to calm your inner critic and raise your authentic voice is to embrace the strengths you were born with. They're part of your DNA and so ingrained, you don't even have to think about them. They simply feel, well, *authentic*. That's because they're all about the best of you.

> **The most natural way to calm your inner critic and raise your authentic voice is to embrace the strengths you were born with.**

I've been asked, "MaryAnn, what if I never find my authentic voice? What if my inner critic just won't let go?"

I love that question, and my response is always the same. Of course, you'll find your authentic voice. It isn't lost. Never was. In fact, it's been a part of your core being since before you were born. Your authenticity is part of who you were created to be. And don't worry about your inner critic not letting go. They're not the one holding on. *You've been holding onto your inner critic.* Whoa, that's a lot to take in. I'll say that again for the folks in the back of the room. *You've been holding onto your inner critic.* You can choose to let go. That's completely within your control, not determined by your circumstances—past or present.

The simple answer to the "but how" question is that your authentic voice is the ultimate truth teller. Its insights can show you where your inner critic is digging in its heels and triggering you to over-express your strengths, such as perfectionism and comparison to others. For me, overusing my Responsibility®, Discipline®, Significance®, and Competition® kept me chasing an unattainable ideal instead of attaining goals. Perfectionism can also be an under-expression of my Intellection®, pushing me to overthink and critique what's required for excellence in serving what matters to me, shift my focus from helping others, and distrusting my common sense. Wherever those imbalances show up for you, Authentic You knows just what you can do to realign with your purpose.

Your strengths will lead you to the truth of you and the excellence inside if you're willing to take positive action. Doing so creates trust in your authentic voice as your consummate truth teller. You'll sense a "knowing" deep within. It will whisper to you when you're being phony. This voice calls you out when your inner critic convinces you to imitate someone else's way of doing things. Heed that whisper of, "Wait a minute. Remember who *you* are." Take the hint. Turn your back on your inner critic and step toward your strong, fearless, unique self.

Recognizing your authentic voice and re-attuning it could be simpler than you've imagined. Try this: Remember back to a time when you felt the most like You. You felt good…really good. You may have to reach back to early childhood. Think about what age you were and what you were doing then. Don't search for a perfect time. Perfection is the myth of your inner critic.

Allow your mind to float back to the time you were happiest just being You. You were Authentic You from the inside out, and you could soar. You felt strong and capable. As you remember, close your eyes. Remember. Enjoy that memory.

Invite that smile on your face from back then to reach your lips now. Feel the corners of your mouth turn up. Yes. There you are! Authentic You. You're on your way there again—only better this time. You're wiser. You picked up this book, didn't you? Keep that smile and keep reading. It's about to get even better.

Green-eyed Monster

Have you ever been jealous? I mean soooo jealous you cried your mascara off? Okay, for the guys, uh, I dunno—cried until your nose ran down into your mustache? I have. One of my creative outlets is stage acting. I've appeared in Shakespeare's plays, contemporary drama and comedy, and there was that appearance in *Oklahoma!* (Musicals aren't my forté. Not good for me and certainly not for the audience. But they really wanted this certain dress in the show, and I was the only one it fit. I 'sang' in the chorus and spent two hours being danced—a.k.a. dragged-up and down the prairie).

Then, along came an audition for a part on my bucket list; I wanted to perform this character so badly. I prepared a ton to make the role mine, employing every device and skill I'd learned from every acting class I'd taken. I thought I had a great shot at getting the role. Putting myself out there had taken courage and vulnerability. My audition had been complimented by other very accomplished actors whose opinions I admired. I was so proud of stretching myself and going for it.

But when the cast list was sent out, I wasn't chosen for the part. In fact, my name wasn't listed for any part. Not even the 'girl holding water pitcher stage left' type of part. I had to read the email three times. *Wait? What? NOT—me? Not—ME? What the h-e-double hockey sticks…?! What did I do wrong? Why not ME?* I was hurt… Really hurt. The pain was palpable.

So, I wallowed. Wallowing continued into the next evening from the cocoon of a warm bubble bath with popcorn and Prosecco and a hefty entreé of Pity. Wallowing soon morphed into jealousy. *A lot* of jealousy. Comparing myself on every level I could digress to. Trust me, there are many levels.

On the outside, I took in the consolation of close friends. Heck, I even found myself being gracious and helpful by volunteering backstage. I was still the sweet, charming southern girl I was raised to be. *Whew.* All better.Yay me! Right?!

Around the same time, I conducted a self-awareness survey and asked ten of my friends who would be candid to name three adjectives that came to mind when they thought of me. I loved their responses. The responses included gracious, confident, focused, respectful, trustworthy, beautiful, caring, organized, driven, strong-willed, witty, bold, clever, supportive, and intelligent. Wow. I knew there was a reason I was friends with these people. So astute. Talk about helping me rebound. Everything was all better.

A few weeks later, and quite unexpectedly, while helping during a rehearsal, the green-eyed monster slithered her way back into my heart and mind. This time she came much better armed. On top of her recent jab, "You're incompetent, untalented, and a whining poser," she added the quite effective, "*And* you're not gracious, neither sweet, nor charming. Just who are you kidding? You know it should have been you all along receiving the 'well done' and 'congratulations.' *Not her*." Gulp. Yeah. The inner critic plays for keeps.

My friend, Cheryl, noticed something seemed "off" with me. Through tears, I shared my struggle. The pain was still there. Why couldn't I just let it go and move on? "In the grand scheme of life, 'this' doesn't matter," I said. It's not like I have dreams of Broadway. (Okay, maybe a little). I asked her, "So what was wrong with me?!"

Her reply stopped me in my tracks: "Why should the tears and the pain you're feeling now be any less significant than the ones you shed over the loss of your mom? You're a compassionate, creative woman. You stepped out of your comfort zone, took a big risk, and it hurt when things didn't turn out the way you'd hoped. I admire the hell out of you." She was right. I have emotions. Some are good, and some are less so. When they're honest and raw, their lessons are powerful.

I've built a company coaching people to live from a place of God-given strengths as their highest and best authentic self. I even named my business AuthenticA. It's what I'm about. Living in fearless authenticity. But what happened when I couldn't handle what I perceived as the weaker parts of my genuine self? I went down the path of self-recrimination. I knew the part well.

Patsy had cast me in a powerless, self-critical role on my life's stage many times before. Of course, Shakespeare wrote something pithy on the topic: "All the world's a stage, And all the men and women merely players." In *As You Like It*, Jaques delivers that line along with a description of the parts we play throughout our lives, illustrating how empty life is when we're just doing what we think we "should" do to be accepted.

Being authentic brings us closer to the glorious and unique parts of ourselves—our best roles we're perfectly suited for—so we can make genuine connections with our brothers and sisters of mankind. We need those who know and love us best to show us the mirror of acceptance, where we see a reflection of our true selves in all their luster of "more than enough."

Calming the Inner Critic

Your authentic voice is your greatest, most powerful tool for calming your inner critic. Why? Because the inner critic hijacks your amazing qualities just enough to make you pause and consider, "Hmmmm." With no push back, the inner critic is emboldened to push further until you're not only questioning the validity of your authentic voice, but you're agreeing with the inner critic's false view of you. Your mind zeroes in on their false, fear-mongering words.

But in strengths mode, your authentic voice can ring out powerfully, revealing the inner critic's half-truths and distorted shreds of your truth. Shown to be a fraud, the inner critic will be left with only that which you allow. While I can't promise that your inner critic will ever completely leave you alone, you can minimize its roar to the faint grumblings simply because it no longer has much to roar about. Its anxiety about you is calmed as your inner knowing recognizes your authentic voice's empowering words as the truth. One of the most important ways your authentic voice does that is by reeling the inner critic in when it's tempted to make us feel and act like a victim.

My colleague, certified EFT coach and award-winning author, Sandy Evenson, writes about getting out of victim mode in her book, *The Woo-Woo Way*. She describes a long-suffering marriage where she felt silent and stayed small, with an alcoholic combat veteran living with undiagnosed PTSD. She felt trapped until one night when he was rushed to the hospital. At that moment, she writes, "[that] traumatic answer to my fretful whispered cry for help forced me to choose. I knew I had to show up... Ultimately, something deep within me was shifting, exposing a tiny bit of inner strength, self-courage, and the taste of freedom to me." Just as she decided to listen to her authentic voice and stand up for herself, when you acknowledge your inborn strengths, you can choose not to act like a victim.

To get a handle on this process, the next time you're tempted to agree with the inner critic's pity party, stand up straight, take a deep breath, and say "*No*. That's wrong. That's a lie. I know the strengths I possess. I know the authentic me. And I love me." Lock arms with Authentic You. Remind yourself of your strengths and how they're uniquely enlivened in you. The more you practice this approach to strengths-based self-leadership, your heart, mind, and voice will follow and regulate your inner critic accordingly. Authentic You thrives in harmony and alignment.

With a calm inner critic, you attain a security of self that gives you the boldness to discover and embrace your purpose.

With a calm inner critic, you attain a security of self that gives you the boldness to discover and embrace your purpose. Do this by honoring your authentic voice to change the patterns in your life that feel limiting or untrue to Authentic You. For example, want to stop feeling like you're being taken advantage of? Notice how you feel next time you're asked for a "little favor." What's the boundary that your strengths require to stay in alignment with the healthiest version of you? We should help each other, but each request and task isn't your responsibility. Do you genuinely want to get involved? What will you have to give less attention to if you say yes? If your answer is no, remember that "No" is a complete sentence.

Be kind and firm if your boundary is pushed; otherwise, your inner critic may not let you hear the end of what was wrong with your boundary and why you shouldn't have needed it. With a calm inner critic, you may train others to respect your new limits, especially if you've trained them to hear "Yes." Avoid over-explaining or justifying yourself. Simply say, "No, I'm not available." People have a right to live inside their own experience and do the work to get to their own highest and best. Your 'no' just might be the best thing you can do for them, and that's something to feel great about. No need to beat yourself up.

But how can your inner critic remain chilled out if you need to make an ask? Observe how you feel to be the one with a need. Do you view it as a weakness? What if you flipped the script and instead saw your request as a multiplier of combining with another person's talents and capacity? We're meant to function in relationship to the world around us and its people. 'Better together' is a phrase you've no doubt heard. Embrace it and embrace others' strengths. For the right people, you need what *they* were born to do.

Watch for inner critic flare-ups in scenarios where you aren't as knowledgeable; see that you come from a place of curiosity instead of defeat. As you choose your behavior in those situations, do you feel energized, which is strengths-based, or deflated, which is fear-based? You get to choose how you respond. Take note of the difference between veering off-course when your inner critic pulls you into a vortex, versus following your authenticity, where no matter the outcome, you feel confident and secure. Be mindful of which voice you're listening to and how it affects what you say, do, and feel.

Aligning your intentions and actions with Authentic You will create positive momentum toward your goals and leave your inner critic in the dust. The point isn't to avoid difficult situations but instead to stop resisting when your personal growth is reaching for a new mountain top and the climb gets steep. And... guess what? You can do hard things (yes, even *you*). I bet you have a list of challenges you have overcome in your life. Maybe now is the time to add some new ones and pursue them fearlessly.

The Truths of Fearless Authenticity

Your degree of "fearlessness" directly correlates to the amount of control your inner critic holds over you; more fearless authenticity means less listening to the inner critic. Hold that ratio in favor of your authenticity, and in time, it becomes easier to maintain. Likewise, hiking, going to the gym, and practicing yoga may begin as chores, but with repetition, you feel healthier and stronger, and those habits become part of how you *do you*. Eventually, you can't imagine your week without working out. Same here.

Sooner than later, you'll be standing firm as The Leader in your own life, summiting your mountains. No more decreed trails. The very thought of caving into your inner critic's taunting will seem so unlike you that it's ridiculous. She'll try to whisper in your ear, and you'll flick her off your shoulder. Fearless authenticity can become a lifestyle of freedom for you, as it has for me.

When unleashing my unique howl and developing my fearless authenticity routine, some important truths came into focus and became an integral part of my way of being. I have written these out as four general truths because my clients have resonated with them so strongly. Perhaps you will, too.

First, living in fearless, unapologetic authenticity is the most honest you can ever be with yourself. Clear alignment with your authenticity means staying in integrity with your heart, soul, mind, and body. And that's as life-changing as it gets, my fine, courageous friend.

Second, authenticity feels easy because you're playing to your strengths. Chasing someone else's version of the good life will keep you exhausted, always climbing uphill with no end in sight. Imitating someone else requires so much energy because it isn't genuine. Being real means more energy is available to maximize your strengths.

Third, authenticity brings with it sustainable joy. You can experience joy now instead of waiting until everything is perfect (which will never happen anyway, since it's a myth). Although unhappy circumstances will occur, and conflicts will still arise, sticking with your authentic voice will keep you aligned with your values and your purpose. Your joy remains intact, regardless of external factors.

Fourth, when you lead with authenticity, you make space for vulnerability, so others may join you. Encouraging others to calm their inner critic and stand fearlessly in their authenticity creates freedom for you, too. When we listen to each other's authentic voices, we learn so much more. Our bonds are strengthened, and we build trust for others we've met on the journey to have our backs when the going gets tough. Climbing higher is safer and much more rewarding when we have traveling companions.

Living out the truths of fearless authenticity requires you to make some changes. You'll encounter some pushback and challenges. A family member or close friend may ridicule a choice you make. Your path may take you in the opposite direction of where you thought you were going. Your circle of relationships may become smaller. Some doors may close in your face. And there will be a few doors you'll need to close. Some will be easier than others. Don't discount the power and support your strengths will provide to keep your destination in focus—your true North.

A critical component of your journey is the agency you give yourself by persevering. Keep going. Because of your unique strengths, what's difficult for me will be simpler for you. And vice versa. But I know you're up for the challenge. How do I know? I've been where you are. I've heard all the lies about myself. And I made up my mind to see, and step into, the truth of who I am and what I'm meant for—my true North. Your inner critic may whisper—or shout—a dozen reasons why you can't do this. That's exactly when you'll need to raise your authentic voice and howl, "Oh, yes, I can! I know the truth of who I am! Imperfect *and* incredible!"

Taking one step up the mountain at a time, one challenge at a time is your success strategy. Focus on the next step. Not getting to the peak. When responding this way to challenges becomes your daily routine, you'll feel the weight of your inner critic lighten and her voice become faint. All you'll hear at the top of the mountain is your triumphant victory howl. *Aaaaa-oooooo!*

Shanna's Story

Shanna went from a daily grind with her inner critic to cultivating her fearless authenticity. She was a very successful hair stylist with Aveda, with a dream to own her own high-end salon. She had invested *everything*, her life savings, her blood, sweat, and tears, sacrificed time with her family into getting it off the ground. And her dream happened, but she was miserable.

She approached me after one of my in-person workshops. "MaryAnn, I can't do this anymore. I've been a victim of my inner critic in more ways than one. I don't want to live like this anymore." She took a breath and in a quivering voice asked, "Can you help me?"

I knew I could. And more importantly, I knew she had everything inside of her to help herself. We made a plan for her to take the CliftonStrengths® assessment and scheduled her first coaching session. I smiled as I looked into her beautiful and tired eyes and said, "Your inner critic's days are numbered." I knew she didn't believe me... yet. And that was okay. I remembered what it was like "before."

She had built up a substantial clientele. Her services were in high demand, and expansion was on the horizon. The work was hard, yet she kept taking the next step, and her business was growing. But a nightmare client was draining her energy and enthusiasm. Every time the woman came in, Shanna felt her blood pressure rise. This client always wanted top-shelf results at an outlet mall price. She'd disagree during the consultation, ask for a less expensive option that she was cautioned wouldn't produce her dream outcome, and then be dissatisfied with the results. After each appointment came the phone call that 'this' or 'that' was wrong with her hair, insisting Shanna "fix it." For free, of course.

Once, this client even expected Shanna to come in over Christmas break. A few years passed, and Shanna began to lose confidence in herself, even though she was an exceptionally gifted hair stylist, always in high demand with a waitlist to get in her chair. She dreaded every time that client's name appeared on the schedule. The woman was becoming more passive-aggressive, and each appointment left Shanna feeling smaller.

When she finally talked to me about it, she was in tears. She wasn't even sure she wanted to keep going at all. Shanna asked, "Are other clients thinking the same thing but not voicing it?" The situation was affecting how she viewed all of her abilities. She was already exhausted running the business and working to expand. The negative voice inside her head, sounding very much like her nightmare client, was making her unsure if she wanted to keep it going at all.

This wasn't the first time Shanna had dealt with that negative voice we all have inside our head. But this time her inner critic had been activated to an even higher decibel by one whose words and actions had taken her back to her youth when she felt she was less than and spent her time trying to be enough for everyone else.

I noticed that Shanna had Futuristic as a top theme. So, I asked her, "What does the future of your business look like? And does the future you envision include this type of client?"

She blew her nose. Without hesitation, she answered with a resounding, "No." She even sat up a little straighter in her chair.

We discussed how to best utilize her other strengths to give her the support she needed. She came up with a kind but firm exit plan. She "broke up" with the client and hasn't looked back.

By implementing her strengths at their highest functioning—the balcony level—she can now succeed on her terms. At a subsequent session, she remarked, "Because of applying my strengths intentionally every day, I feel empowered to make decisions that positively impact my life and work. That helps me to positively impact others. I don't resent my business anymore. Instead, I look forward to what each day holds."

Since calming her inner critic through a strengths-based mindset, Shanna is leading herself and her team with more confidence. People travel from other cities to her salon, which is on track for another banner year. She gets up in the morning excited for what each day holds and recently celebrated the salon's ninth anniversary. And drumroll... the salon was invited to be stylists at Paris Fashion Week this past spring.

So, if you've had the wind knocked out of you like Shanna, then get up. Go toe-to-toe with your inner critic by realizing the power of your unique strengths. While you're at it, make the most of them by serving your corner of the world the way only you can. Your strengths-based, fearless authenticity will bring your purpose calling from deep inside to life.

What if Things Weren't—Perfect?

The simplest way I've found to explain the transformation into living with fearless authenticity comes from *Hamlet.* Shakespeare writes, "To thine own self be true." I've continued to learn that lesson long since my first full howl.

One particular learning came early in my business. Several days after making a social media post that got views, likes, and comments, I looked at it again. The word *"authenticity"* was misspelled.

With lightning speed, my inner critic was off to the races. I mean, Patsy could hardly breathe; she was cackling so hard. She shouted, "What an idiot. Like, who's going to trust you to help them find their authentic voice when you can't even spell the word? For Pete's sake—*it's the name of your company.* Everyone's rolling their eyes and laughing at you. I mean... good luck growing your brand!"

She was well on her way to dragging me back to the fourth grade playground when Ethan Johnson nailed me in the face with a dodgeball, and everyone roared with laughter. I was crying and in pain in more ways than one as my cheek swelled up. But this time, something happened in the middle of feeling humiliated.

My authentic self squared her shoulders back and grabbed Patsy by her greasy pig tails and tossed her off the playground of my mind. I decided then and there to lean into the fearless part of my authenticity. *What would it feel like if things weren't—perfect?* I ignored the shrieks inside my head and fearlessly tested what making mistakes, even public ones, felt like.

I did not correct the misspelling.

Not one person mentioned the mistake. I'm not sure if that's a symptom of our education system these days, but the next time you make an embarrassing public mistake, just roll with it. Get up, dust yourself off, and get an ice pack for the welt on your face. You'll be okay; in fact, you'll be 1000x better than okay. Because you're being fearless, authentic you. And that's better than anything.

You can change from the old, dark, disjointed patterns, begin stitching together your vibrant qualities, and create your life anew. With each stitch, you'll become attuned to the sound of your authentic voice, and like a soft quilt, your self-knowing and self-advocacy will envelope you. In this next, final chapter of *The Howl of the Whisper,* you'll put together the self-knowledge you've gained to build your four cornerstones of authentic self-leadership, presenting a united front to keep your inner critic at bay. Before we get there, do a little work on the substance from this chapter to keep your forward momentum. You're doing great work.

Meet me at Pause & Practice for Chapter 5 in the back of the book.

6

SELF-LEADERSHIP

Know Thyself

One of the most meaningful jobs of my life was with a nonprofit that worked closely with the obscenity task forces of the FBI and the Department of Justice. I felt called to fight for those damaged by the sex industry. Childhood experiences with my predator had taught me that pornography led to obscenity, and obscenity led to harmful choices. The work was daunting, dark, and beyond difficult most days. I knew but for the grace of God, I could have ended up like any of the women I worked so hard to help.

Children don't dream of being objectified and abused. The tolls on one's heart, soul, mind, and body are excruciating. That stress can manifest itself in a myriad of destructive choices. How do you cope when your humanity and dignity are pillaged as the spoils of a depraved aggressor? The list of options for self-destruction is, unfortunately, long. The 'little girls grown up' that I encountered lived in survival mode, trapped in a hamster wheel of fight, flight, or freeze.

Fortunately, the work was meaningful, and we made a difference. Did we save everyone? You already know the answer. We did not. However, like the story of the starfish, we did save some. It's one of my favorite stories. A young girl was walking along a beach upon which thousands of starfish had been washed up during a terrible storm. As she approached each starfish, she picked it up and gently threw it back into the ocean.

After some time, a man approached her. He said, "Little girl, what are you doing? Look at this beach. You can't save all these starfish. You can't begin to make a difference."

She was crushed and deflated. Then, she spied another starfish, bent down, picked it up, and hurled it as far as she could into the ocean. She looked up at the man and replied, "Well, I made a difference for that one."

I've often wondered how many more children there were just like me during those terrible years, suffocating in fear and waiting for someone to rescue them. As an adult, I was that rescuer throwing as many precious starfish back into the ocean as I could. The weight of the day-in and day-out toil became more than I could bear. My mother had most noticed the cloud forming around me and suggested I "do something fun for a change."

Just as the girl in the story left the beach eventually, I reluctantly had to leave the obscenity task force, too. At that time, my spouse had recently retired from the Army, and we moved from Fort Knox to our home in Shelby County, Kentucky. It's a beautiful part of the Bluegrass State, and I was excited to still be close to my beloved Appalachian Mountains to visit, hike, and go creek trompin' whenever I wish.

My new hometown of Shelbyville is home to an award-winning regional playhouse. (I mentioned it earlier in Chapter 5). Shortly after our move, one afternoon, I drove down Main Street and saw the sign—Shelby County Community Theatre. Mom's words to do something "fun" came back to me. During my difficult high school years, one of the bright spots was drama class with Mrs. Beulah Back. I don't even remember any names of the plays we produced, but I do remember feeling at home on the stage. I'd also enjoyed being on the drama team at a couple of churches and loved telling stories to bring them to life.

Acting requires you to be emotionally vulnerable. You can feel exposed, especially when aspects of your character resonate deeply with you, the actor. One of our directors, the brilliant Dr. Jack Wann, is masterful at teasing out those connection points and contrasts to propel you into the authenticity of bringing art to life on the stage. Conditions are generally very ripe for the inner critic to pipe up.

Soon after joining the acting company, I realized that my inner critic found a whole new playground to skip around on. While I loved immersing myself into my character, before being cast, I had to audition. Before I even walked into the audition space, I would begin to feel the weight of Patsy on my back. Afterward, I'd wait for the cast list to be announced, and Patsy would come at me in full force.

Finally, the cast list would be posted. Sometimes my name was listed for the role I wanted, sometimes for another role, and other times not at all. (Remember the green-eyed monster scenario—*ick*). Any time I wasn't cast into a particular role, I would spiral, taking it as a personal rejection of my worth. Soooooo, getting the part should solve all that, right? Wrong.

Let's say that I have the part. *Yikes. Holy Crap. What have I done? Can I do this? Everyone else has so much more experience; they're better than me.* Before going on stage, during a scene, or catching a glimpse of someone who wasn't cast sitting in the audience, my inner critic would whisper, "They're all gonna see you fail," "You botched that scene," or "You always screw up that same line. What's wrong with you?" And the clincher was: "The director is probably thinking she made a mistake casting you." The whispers turned into howls when I allowed the inner critic to pull me out of character, even for a split second. My focus would shift from living authentically in the moment of the scene to being an observer, having undermined the confidence of my character.

I wasn't about to let Patsy ruin my fun. So, I leaned hard into what I coach my clients toward—authentic self-leadership. It's best described in Act 1, Scene 3 of Shakespeare's *Hamlet*. Polonius advises his son who's leaving home for university, "... To thine own self be true, And it must follow, as the night the day, Thou canst not then be false to any man." Gendered language aside, our self-leadership is measured by how authentically we both live in the truth of who we were created to be and express our truth to others. We do that best with our inner critic's microphone powered "off."

Instead of listening to the whispers of "You'll never be as good as her" or "He's a real actor. You're just faking it, and sooner or later, everyone will figure it out," I doubled down on what I knew to be true about Patsy's tricks. She loved comparison because it fueled my tendency toward impostor syndrome. To strike back and shut Patsy up, when I saw someone else succeeding, I allowed that as proof that I was talented enough to do the same. I began taking acting classes and eventually private acting coaching.

Putting in the work and instilling solid tools are essential strategies to set yourself on a growth path. I leaned into my acting strengths just as I had done at work and in dealing with my daughter's stroke. Now, when feedback and direction are given to me in rehearsal, I'm more likely to hear that my potential is being stretched, and they believe I can get this character right. This is intended to help me grow into the actor I strive to be. I find it ironic that in wanting to empower people to control their inner critic, I chose a passion project like acting. It has certainly given me invaluable research and insights. Few people on the planet are more self-critical than actors.

You may be wondering how acting relates to authenticity when following a script seems like the very opposite of being genuine. But when done with talent and a desire to tell your character's truth, acting becomes a mechanism to authentically express aspects of myself I might've otherwise never known. Instead of putting on the mask of a character, I've learned to experience, in real time, what my character is experiencing and feeling–be it grief, love, anger, or joy. I notice the self-leadership traits my characters possess or lack, and I search for how I'm similar. Drawing on my emotional well of past experiences, joys, and traumas helps me grow as an actor and as an imperfect human navigating the world from a place of strength, peace, and joy.

Authentic Self-Leadership

Authentic self-leadership isn't only about being true to yourself but also allowing the truth of another's strengths to be equal to or greater than your own. We recognize and respect the individual humanity in ourselves and everyone else. As we expand our emotional and moral curiosity, self-leadership prompts us to embrace a higher level of self-complexity, which in turn enables us to do the same for others. The best leaders have this capacity. As Malala Yousafzai says, "I raise up my voice—not so I can shout, but so that those without a voice

> **Authentic self-leadership isn't only about being true to yourself.**

can be heard." Thank you, Malala. And Mel Robbins offers great motivation toward that purpose: "You have been assigned this mountain so that you can show others it can be moved." When your purpose is at stake, self-leadership is required.

Fearlessly authentic self-leadership requires intense self-reflection. Bold choices, such as admitting our weaknesses and owning our strengths, are a hallmark of authentic self-leadership. This inner work calls us to address, or dare I say, confront, parts of ourselves we may have never seen before and those we don't want to acknowledge. This requires vulnerability because our self-knowledge that arises isn't always pleasant, nor should we expect it to be. (Take heart in this because... *Life is messy*. We have messes, and those we interact with have their messes).

Showing vulnerability and owning our flaws and mistakes can guide us to the highest, most authentic iteration of ourselves—the "who" that we were created to be. That was driven home during my early theatre years when I auditioned for a character in a well-known Broadway hit, *Steel Magnolias*. I was thrilled to be cast as M'Lynn. Until panic set in. *What have I done? I can't do this. The other actors in the ensemble are so talented, so experienced, so...* During the second rehearsal, one of my castmates took me aside and said, "Look. You auditioned. You got the part. Stop whining and take responsibility. You wanted it. You got it. *We* all know you can do it. So. Do. It." She was exactly right. The same voice inside me that gave me what I needed to audition and convince the director to cast me would catapult me to success in the role. And it did. One of my favorite roles to date.

Overthinking and second-guessing ourselves can run rampant without solid self-leadership to stand up to the negative thoughts. If a thought like, "what a stupid choice" pops in, we can take all the air out of it by finding the lesson of what we might do better next time. Or we may answer the critic that we did our best with the tools available to us at the time. At other times, we may feel called to be greater and hear whispers that, "You're not creative enough," or "Don't go there. You'll just embarrass yourself." If we don't stand up against self-doubt, firm in our strengths, the inner critic will waste no time distorting a jolt of courage into an unsafe risk.

Leading with authenticity requires us to align our inner strengths with our outward presence. Even that changes when we embrace our natural strengths, guide our life choices by what we want and don't want, and then show up each day fully present in fearless authenticity. We do so regardless of what others think, how they do things, or what they approve of or not; instead, we let go and trust ourselves. I don't mean that we're abrasive; the goal is to be firm in who we are.

The inner work of self-leadership is kryptonite to the inner critic, and the more of it we do, the stronger our resilience when the critic pipes up. Before now, you were often stuck or quickly shoved down the yuck. *Not this time.* You can increase inner truth and deepen self-healing with each thwarted blow. That's the last thing Patsy ever wanted me to do. And I'm so glad I did it anyway. Being real, Authentic You is where your creativity and genius lie.

David's Story

When you commit to a higher level of strengths-based self-leadership, you present yourself differently, you interact differently, and genuine confidence rises. The result is alchemy of the highest form. Then, your followers may sense your self-trust, and they may, in turn, feel more confident and trust you with more of their authenticity. Your capacity provides space for others and their authentic strengths, compounding the collective positive force of your team.

One of the best examples of authentic self-leadership I've seen is my client, David. I met him because we are both stage actors. He was the Director of Innovative Learning at the Kentucky Department of Education, where a primary focus was high-level self-leadership and high-quality development of his team. Often, David and I chatted about work before rehearsal, and he had some prior knowledge of Gallup's CliftonStrengths®.

One day, he lamented, "Today was the weekly Monday morning all-hands meeting. But I was surrounded by human crickets. Sometimes they won't say anything. Every week before the meeting, I ask myself, 'What in the world is it going to take to get these people talking and brainstorming?'" He did a double-take at me and added, "Could your group coaching help?"

"I believe so," I said. "Strengths work guides everyone to be who they are at their best and use that to manage where we struggle."

He shared that an influx of work was finding its way to his desk, and he couldn't decide how to delegate it. He was overwhelmed. "My team is great, and I don't want to put people in the wrong places, have them not be successful, the work suffer, and they end up frustrated."

That 'overwhelm' was David's inner critic stopping by for a visit with a carry-on bag of self-doubt. And the visits were becoming more frequent. Up to this point in his career, he considered himself a pretty traditional supervisor. (I should note here that "traditional supervisors" aren't always self-aware, much less this forward-thinking). But leave it to David and his Innovative Learner strength to *always be improving on the status quo* and to seek a new tool when his old ones weren't working.

I structured a strengths-based coaching program for David and his team over one year. He especially wanted me to focus on one person who was always saying, "but" during meetings—much to David's chagrin. We discovered that all the staff members had talent in Futuristic Thinking, except the person who seemed completely opposite from the group; their talent was Context®. After strengths-based coaching, David saw how this team member's strength saved the team valuable resources and often prevented frustrations. "Now, I'm thankful for those *buts*!"

Remember how David felt overwhelmed by his division's increased workload and how he didn't want to let them down or cause frustration? Once armed with Strengths knowledge of himself and his staff, he strategized delegation with ease and confidence. He aligned his goals with his values and aspirations for his team and their vital work. And the result? He said, "Our team is functioning at a much higher level and our productivity has skyrocketed!"

He experienced self-leadership alchemy at its finest. As he put it, "When your leader is able to identify and position you perfectly to lean into your strengths—that's where the *real* magic happens! The entire team picks up steam and begins moving forward like a well-oiled machine." Because David was confident in who he was and he wanted that for his team members, they felt more self-confident and freer to share their thoughts. Ideas, once stifled, now flowed.

The transformation around David extended into a local school system he worked with. One superintendent had his teachers, staff, students, parents—everyone—have their strengths assessed. Consider how, in most schools, broadening the mind should be the goal; instead, students are taught not to expand beyond preset boundaries. They're encouraged to blend in. Meld. Conform. Find that box and fit yourself inside it–the very opposite of authentic self-leadership. Well, these kids found comfort and pride knowing that their unique strengths are their superpowers. Just imagine what's possible if we can get that nasty inner critic to be quiet in childhood and the teenage years. *Life-changing.*

The personal and professional benefits of strengths-based coaching are undeniable. Today, David has retired and continues to lead his company, Learning Ecosystem Design, where he remains passionate about empowering youth with the incredible methodology of CliftonStrengths. He was so inspired; he became a Gallup® certified CliftonStrengths coach and supports school districts and state education agencies across the country.

The Four Cornerstones of Self-Leadership

As we navigate our world of rapid change, noise, turmoil, dissent, and endless demands on our time and attention, we may feel as if we're barely treading water in our own lives. Maybe you're also a "boss" over agendas, never-ending tasks, and the people assigned to them, and your workplace feels like a quagmire at times. While blaming the world (and the annoying people in it) for our troubles might seem

> **The only winning strategy to end what's raging on the outside is to go within and become our own authentic self-leader.**

satisfying, it rarely produces positive change. The only winning strategy to end what's raging on the outside is to go within and become our own authentic self-leader. *No ifs, ands, or buts.*

We must stop finger-pointing and clarify what truly matters to us—and what limiting beliefs are clouding our self-perspective.

To step out of the daily drama and do this inner work, we must arm ourselves with the strategic, strengths-based Four Cornerstones of Self-Leadership. They are: #1 Discovery and Understanding, #2 Accountability, #3 Growth, and #4 Agility. Aim these directly toward your goals, aligning your words and actions with your truth, and hold yourself accountable for your hits and misses. Every decision, behavior, and aspiration stems from somewhere, whether we recognize it or not. Keep practicing to become ever-increasingly agile and resilient. We may not perfectly accept all our facets all the time, but we can invite ourselves to further align with them during each season of our evolving purpose.

#1 Discovery and Understanding

Of course, the starting point of self-leadership is to discover your strengths so you can understand the amazing human you are. (If you haven't taken the assessment yet, why not just go ahead, and I'll stop reminding you). Your strengths reveal insights into what makes you feel most alive, what you're willing to take a stand on even when it's hard, and the values you draw upon when making your best decisions. With this awareness, you may identify the meanings you assigned to some core events of your life as ringing false.

Now, we all have our "stories." I don't mean the kind my grandmother used to watch on her black & white television propped up on a rickety TV tray, but the unconscious stories the inner critic tells, which, left unchecked, define who we are and what we believe is possible for our lives. For instance, perhaps we feel unable to speak up because our parents wanted us to be "seen and not heard." We stayed quiet then to survive, but why, as adults, do we often still fear punishment for using our voice?

Part of developing authentic self-leadership is diving into those stories, challenging their validity, and changing the channel on the ones that no longer serve us. (Here's a bonus insight for you—if your inner critic is still whispering it in your ear or shouts it from time to time, you can guarantee it's BS. Turn the dial to another frequency).

Several of my clients came to me devaluing their ideas and contributions. Often, unconsciously or outright, they avoided opportunities to step forward and speak up. After a little discovery work with their strengths, a fresh understanding of their uniqueness washes over them, providing the strength to stand firm in their values. Then they examine the origin of their limiting beliefs, recognize the truth, and reframe the story they tell themselves into an empowering refrain, such as: "I lead in my way that is authentic to my sense of integrity to myself and others."

There's no way to understand who you are except through self-awareness. It's achieved through the regular, ongoing practice of tuning into your thoughts, emotions, and behaviors to sift the negative activators from the positive ones. Self-awareness allows you to notice patterns of negative self-talk, catch limiting beliefs before they can take a foothold, and change course with positive intention. Meditation, journaling, coaching, and feedback from *trusted* colleagues and friends are all vital to this cornerstone. Self-awareness is not a destination; it's a practice—an agreement to meet yourself from a place of curiosity, conscience, and compassion every day.

#2 Accountability

If you met your Avatar on another planet, would *you* follow you? Would you trust you? If not, changes may be in order in your personal and public life. Apologies made. That's okay. Simply take stock. Respect yourself enough to be in integrity with your inner truth. The cornerstone of accountability demands radical ownership of how we respond to whatever life presents to us.

No defensiveness, no blame… not that we stay in a posture of guilt and self-recrimination (even when we blow it). Instead of exacting self-punishment, we take a hard look at our role in any situation that seems outside our control.

For example, maybe a pivotal team member quit because they're moving out of state to care for their aging parents. Although you wanted to sympathize, you felt rejected after all your mentorship and lashed out at them for leaving you in the lurch with a project. When the dust settles, a deeper truth may emerge—like how you value togetherness in the office and don't permit hybrid work. So, in their situation, you had no compromise to offer, and that's true to you, and it's right and true that their family duties came before work. We unearth the courage of our convictions by drawing a line of accountability in the sand and owning our responses, actions, and choices.

Taking accountability shifts us from feeling out of control to providing us meaningful agency, as in putting us in the driver's seat to design our one and only amazing life. Here, we may change direction if we're careening toward a ravine, instead of acting like deer in the headlights, believing, "I can't help it; it's just the way I am." Even better, we can run simulations of our choices and assess the fallout of things we might say or do beforehand and choose better out of the gate. And when we blow it—which we all do sometimes despite our best efforts—we can reflect, "What was my part in this, and what can I do differently?" A great next step could be apologizing for handling a situation in a manner that falls short of what you now require of yourself. In times when something misses the mark, we're truthful about it, even when fessing up is hard or embarrassing. Our integrity demands no less.

Aligning our integrity and authenticity includes being accountable to ourselves. Plenty of my clients wouldn't dream of not following through on a promise to their customers, so they make those statements with great care. Yet, when promising themselves to wake up early, meditate, go to the gym, or start a new hobby, those resolutions are made flippantly. Doing what we tell our-selves we will do is a game-changing act of self-leadership. We build immense self-trust and self-confidence knowing that we're who we say we are, even when no one would know otherwise.

Self-leadership requires us to be accountable for our emotions, meaning we lead them, not vice versa. Now, you're human. So, am I. We have feelings about events in our lives and things we care about. Sometimes I have very strong feelings. You, too? When our emotions run high, the inner critic does some of its best work—and the most damaging—from inciting our righteous indignation to just plain ole "I'm pissed!"

Emotions are tricky because they're feelings that aren't right or wrong, and denying them just makes your inner critic's day because then you're out of integrity with yourself. Emotions just are. Yet, we're accountable for our reactions. So, we must cultivate our personal character to allow feelings like anger or disappointment to "be" without showing up as a lesser version of ourselves. Through practicing the positive expression of our strengths and values, along with the first two cornerstones of self-leadership, we become formidably self-possessed. Through understanding ourselves, our old feelings, and our patterns of reaction, we may *respond* with the desired positive outcome in mind rather than *react* in the heat of the moment.

Always remember that in your humanness, old feelings and patterns can be activated, but they don't have to cause you to behave badly. That's your choice. We are all responsible for how we choose to respond. When you may wish you'd responded better, don't let your inner critic have the last word. Put Patsy back in her place by showing yourself grace, staying account-able to make it right, and learning the lesson for next time. What went wrong? What choice will I make next time? Discuss your options with a mentor, coach, or trusted friend. Make amends. This level of proactive accountability and behavior modification empowers you to move out of blame and self-shame and into clarity and self-compassion.

#3 Growth

When was the last time you stretched beyond your comfort zone? Self-leadership demands that we never settle into comfort or complacency. To grow, we must extend beyond what we think we know or can do. Authentic self-leaders seek experiences that will stretch them, even if it means discomfort, embarrassment, or failure. One thing they know for sure is that they won't be saddled one day with rocking chair regret. They keep their eye on their prize. For me, that's howling at the top of Mount Katahdin.

As I write this, I have recently declared to family and friends, and now here to you—*yikes*—that I will train to hike the Appalachian Trail. And when I turn sixty next year, I'll begin my trek. To accomplish that, I can't be complacent nor focused on what's comfortable all the time. Sore feet, possible bears, snakes, and rainstorms, here I come.

To accomplish this bucket list goal, I must stay in a growth mindset and believe I can improve and do hard things. I can do that by leaning on my strengths in brand new ways. How can I use them to support Carla, as we attempt the goal together? Which of your strengths do you think you would use? Learner® already has me researching and consulting with those who know how to best train physically. My Strategic Thinking mindset will help me with a strategy for success. Each of them is ready to help me remember that I can do what I put my mind to in my own unique way.

I keep my strengths at the forefront of all I do, and they help keep me in a growth mindset *and* out of a fixed mindset. We all know people with fixed mindsets. Sometimes all we have to do is look in the mirror. They avoid challenges, give up when it gets hard, and don't learn from their failures. That's all fodder for the inner critic and its desire to trap us in self-doubt and unworthiness. But that's not for you anymore. Since picking up this book, you're learning to embrace tough spots and setbacks as evidence of where to grow further and find inspiration for a greater level of self-leadership. *Exponential self-growth only happens outside of our comfort zone.*

Beware of the comfort zone. That's your inner critic's seductress. Growth-oriented self-leaders are lifetime learners who seek out new information, ask questions, and reflect on the fresh ideas they're discovering. They seek feedback for greater breadth and depth of insight. One significant habit they practice is to listen and learn from people different from themselves, those with what I call 'variant opinions and perspectives.' Self-leaders must trust themselves enough to be open to others' wisdom and expand their thought agility, empathy, and wisdom.

I taught the variant quality recently to an executive leadership team during an organizational mission and goals alignment training. The former CEO was dictatorial in style, and the culture remained permeated with hesitation to speak up despite the new CEO's encouragement. During an exercise to build psychological safety between the new leader and his team, we set up the expectation for 'variant opinions' to be shared. This expectation made space for conversations with him and each other to be just that- conversations with varying thoughts and perspectives. No one had to feel defensive about offering a different idea or solution. Having this occur in private contexts outside of the group provided a training runway, which helped pave the way for variant opinions to be shared inside formal meetings. I hear the culture is transforming through an increase in psychological safety and creativity in problem-solving.

Transformation into an authentic self-leader isn't the result of one decision to make a huge promise to yourself and make a grand gesture to prove it. No. It's the cumulative effect of small, consistent steps over time. In my coaching practice, I call these micro goals. Small. Consistent. Repeated. And again the next day. Once mastered, the next set of micro goals are layered in, and those amalgamate into the larger overarching goal. As you see steady progress in each micro goal, building toward the main objective feels more very doable and substantive. Accountability becomes easier, too. And celebrating the small successes along the way to the bigger victory is more fun.

#4 Agility

Self-leadership demands our resilience to adapt, change course, and thrive in the face of a challenge. I don't mean *tolerating* chaos: Agility connotes the strength and stamina to address life's unpredictability. After all, the only constant is that the world is in a constant state of change, and we adapt to it better by not looking back or putting our heads in the sand. We can answer the inner critic's whispers of uncertainty with the howl of our authentic strengths.

The key to agility is being more concerned with how we can improve things than why a situation arose. The agile mindset says, "I may not have caused the situation, but I possess the leadership qualities to address it." That resilience is the result of all the principles discussed in this book. You can embody a higher level of confidence because you've done the work. So, when the unexpected 'thing' comes, you know you handle it because your inner critic remains calm, and you trust your authentic voice. What a gift your strengths are in a crisis, both to you and those depending on you.

Our call to agility can be more subtle than full-on turmoil. Sometimes influences around us point to a need to reevaluate our lives and goals. A peer's heart attack can make us wonder if we're as healthy as we think. Reading a personal development book like this may stir up uncomfortable questions, and sometimes the stirrings in our soul just demand to be heard. Through calming your inner critic, living in the power and edge of your strengths, and recognizing your authentic voice, you may find that your life feels static. The inner critic likes to keep us there. She's lazy like that. She loves a good comfort zone. The smaller the better. But now you have a great personal advantage over her because you can assess where things may be out of alignment and choose your next actions, without the inner critic butting in.

Greater agility also helps us let go of perfectionism. We can't be successful, contented leaders in our lives or anyone else's if we don't let it go. No single person has all the solutions, or all the right words to keep everyone happy and everything running smoothly and in tip-top shape all the time. Oh, but the inner critic absolutely wants us to think that's our role. If we agree, then it just sits back and lets us beat ourselves up. The inner critic loves to work us into a state of paralysis, so we chase the myth of perfectionism through procrastination. Choose agility over inertia to create forward momentum toward positive change.

Essentially, this cornerstone teaches us to strive for steady and solid progress. The end goal is excellence. This kind of agility and resilience in stressful situations runs circles around the inner critic. And maybe most importantly, those around you will feel the freedom for their authentic voice and integrity in the face of imperfection to rise.

Each cornerstone is an important piece in your stronger foundation to move forward in fearless authenticity. You've discovered your strengths and have a better understanding of how to put them to good use; you're growing and stretching while holding yourself accountable; and you're transforming into an agile and resilient leader who has big plans and what it takes to make them happen. But that doesn't mean we're riding off into the sunset, living "happily ever after."

Some cornerstones may slip from time to time. So, be vigilant that all four are in place to support Authentic You. Your new self needs all of them. Discovery without accountability leads to insight with no actionable purpose. Accountability without growth creates inflexibility and judgment. Growth without agility causes misdirection and burnout. Agility without new practical discoveries leads to a lack of purpose and direction. The best revenge you can serve cold to your inner critic is balancing your cornerstones and living your life aligned in harmony with the howl of your fearless, authentic self. You're coming to the finish line of your effort thus far. As a boost for what's beyond this book, I've got some key practice for you ready to go.

Meet me at Pause & Practice for Chapter 6 in the back of the book.

Conclusion

A Word to the Wise

A client once asked me what to do when her family wasn't supportive of some of the changes she was integrating. Her son openly mocked her efforts. She was crushed.

Here's what I told her: "Some people will never understand why you're doing what you're doing. They're used to the 'old you.' They want you back in their comfort zone, where you stayed in line and never rocked the boat."

In a way, when people resist your change, it's understandable, although very hurtful. Your newfound voice and strength may present in ways that are unfamiliar and may make some people very uncomfortable. Perhaps your transformation may highlight what they aren't doing in their life. Their authentic voice could feel the tension of being muzzled or the new you may feel unfamiliar, and what's unfamiliar can seem scary. Fear can make us feel threatened, and when we're threatened, we can lash out. How they respond may not be pleasant. I've been called a "backslider" for the change in how I practice my faith. I've been shunned from circles that used to welcome me.

I promise, though, calming your inner critic will be an amazing adventure that was *always* meant for you to travel. Cheerleaders (like me) will appear at just the right time, and you'll find guidebooks and resources (like this one) to help you find your way. Fellow travelers charting their new path may join you as they follow the sound of their fearless, authentic voice.

You'll recognize them as being kindred spirits. Believe it or not, you'll support each other on your journeys because you share the value of not turning back. You can't unhear your authentic voice's howl once you've let it permeate your heart, soul, mind, and body.

Step Out with Confidence

I can have that red rain boot feeling any time I choose by embracing and celebrating who I am from the inside out. For me, red means might, vibrance, joy, and resilience. It's bright, cheerful, and confident. During the search for my birth family, I found a document from my time as an infant in foster care. The social worker reported, "Her favorite toy is a red ball. In fact, she really loves any toy with the color red." How cool is that?! The color red and I go back a long way. No doubt that's why it feels so "right," so authentic to the positive energy, strength, and determination I seek in my life.

The stream in my woods goes on for miles and meets up with a much larger creek, which travels even further. I can follow it as far as I want to go. Our lives are similar. How far we go in life, how authentic and meaningful that life becomes, is determined in part by each of us putting on our red rain boots and having the confidence to step out.

I implore you to step beyond the present level of illusory comfort found in your status quo and move upward to the next tier of your one amazing life. You have gifts, talents, and strengths that the rest of us need. Do you hear me? Not only do you deserve to be at the table, but you're also *needed* at the table.

The incredible Marianne Williamson expressed it so perfectly when she wrote her magnificent poem, "Our Deepest Fear." If you've never read it, look it up. It hangs on my office wall, and I want to share part of it with you here:

Our deepest fear is not that we are inadequate.
Our deepest fear is that we are powerful beyond measure…
Your playing small does not serve the world.

Oh my amazing, fine, courageous friend… You are needed. You are valued. You are loved.

Don't turn back. That howl you know you want to let out needs to be released. *Aaaah-oooooo!*

—MaryAnn

Pause & Practice

The exercises in this section coordinate with the book chapters in numerical order.

As you read each chapter, complete its Pause & Practice to apply the concepts and theories in ways that you individually curate.

Chapter 1— Defining Your Personal Success

PAUSE: Find a quiet place where you can reflect. When you're ready, close your eyes and take three deep breaths. With each breath move deeper into your inner knowing of you. Tune your attention there. Take one more deeper breath and hold it for a count of three, then blow it out of your mouth.

Reflect on your natural gifts and talents you know you possess even if it's been awhile since you've brought them forward. Trust your authentic voice to guide you to naming at least one. Open your eyes and move on to the PRACTICE.

PRACTICE: Write below your answer to the following questions. Be honest with yourself no matter where you are in your process.

- What does success look like to you if no one else's opinion mattered? (Here's a freebie to get you started. *No one else's opinion matters. Only yours.*)

  _____

  _____

  _____

  _____

  _____

- What is your best life? Write down everything that comes to mind. There are no rules.

  _____

  _____

  _____

  _____

  _____

- What am I doing consistently to get there? (Here's another freebie—*you're reading this book and putting in the work.*)

  _____

  _____

  _____

  _____

  _____

- Why do you get up in the morning? (This can be tough to answer. Keep it honest. And know that if you don't like the answer, you don't have to stay there. Keep reading.)

  _____

  _____

  _____

  _____

  _____

- When you're eighty-five, what will you wish you had done to avoid rocking chair regret?

  _____

  _____

  _____

  _____

  _____

Chapter 2— Origins of Your Inner Critic

PAUSE: You're probably gonna need a couple more deep breaths for this one so follow the guidance from earlier. You're doing great.

It's time to reflect on the first time you remember hearing a negative voice that got stuck in your head. As hard as this is. Don't avoid it. Breathe and allow it to come up so it can pass through and out.

PRACTICE A: Answer the following questions:

- Whose voice was it?

  _____

- What did they say?

  _____

- How old were you?

  _____

- What was happening at the time?

  _____

PRACTICE B: You don't have to be as talented as Shakespeare here. But do bring your whole heart, whole self to create your new narrative.

Use the space below to write a poem, a song, an essay, jot down a few words for each question, or you can use a different medium such as colored pencils to sketch, sculpture clay, or watercolors to paint, etc.

Choose what feels authentic to you in processing and expressing your thoughts.

- How do I feel I was defined by others' and their choices?
- How was I defined by my decisions to fit in?
- What have I accepted in my life to not feel damaged or dismissed?
- How do I want to begin again and choose anew from this point forward?
- What can I rely on to help me create my authentic life?

Chapter 3— Clarity

This exercise deals with your strengths as identified by Gallup's CliftonStrengths Assessment. If you've chosen not to take the assessment, complete the exercise using the knowledge you have of your natural talents and gifts. To take this assessment pause here and go to https://www.store.gallup.com and select the Top 5 assessment. I do not benefit from your purchase.)

PAUSE: Review your Top 5 results. Highlight, underline, or circle words and phrases that resonate with you. Spend some time with your report and any learning aids that accompany it. Remember that this report is unique to you. There's a 1 in 33 million chance that someone else in the world will have your exact order of Top 5 Strengths. *You're quite special!*

PRACTICE A: I hope you've chosen to take the CliftonStrengths Assessment. If so, list your Top 5 Strengths below. As you do, review each one, making a mental note of the qualities that resonate with you about each of these superpowers. Next to each Strength, jot down what most stands out to you about each strength. Do you remember a time when you first were aware you possessed this ability?

Name of Strength	Qualities	I first realized these qualities at age/when
1.		
2.		
3.		
4.		
5.		

PRACTICE B: After becoming familiar with your results, think about a time during the past few weeks that's an example of your strengths in action.

- How did a particular strength(s) help you in your task, project, or situation? Write about it in the space below.

_____

_____

_____

_____

_____

Chapter 4— Know Thy Enemy

PAUSE: More fun. I know. Ugh. Of all the negative things your inner critic says to you, I want you to think about the five you repeat to yourself the most often. That fuels your Patsy every time you do it. It's time to cut off the power supply.

PRACTICE A: Write down the five negative things you repeat to yourself.

1) _____

2) _____

3) _____

4) _____

5) _____

PRACTICE B: Make this promise to yourself and me.

"I,_____(name), will never contribute to my inner critic again by repeating negative statements to myself. They are lies. I will rid myself of them as I welcome the power of my fearless authentic voice."

Chapter 5— Embracing Authentic You

PAUSE: Finally some fun! You've worked so hard, you deserve it.

Think of 10 people you trust to support you and jot down their names.

PRACTICE: Text the ten people on your list—separately. Not in a group text. Send this message:

"Hey— I'm participating in a self-awareness exercise. Would you please reply within twenty-four hours with the first three adjectives that come to mind when you think of me. Thanks!"

Don't provide any other information.

Write down the responses you receive below-

_____   _____   _____

_____   _____   _____

_____   _____   _____

_____   _____   _____

_____   _____   _____

_____   _____   _____

_____   _____   _____

_____   _____   _____

_____   _____   _____

Chapter 6— Self-Leadership

PAUSE: Spend some time reflecting back on the favorite parts of your CliftonStrengths report and the adjectives you received from the Chapter 5 exercise. Read everything you like out loud to yourself. In front of a mirror is even better.

PRACTICE A: Look back at the five negative statements in the Chapter 4 exercise. (The ones you're never going to repeat again.)

Rewrite each statement below using as many of your new adjectives as you wish for each one.

1) _____

2) _____

3) _____

4) _____

5) _____

PRACTICE B: In the margins, write in which of your Top 5 strengths you'll use to support your new mindset. (Now that's a great use of the margin!)

Final Wrap Up

Don't put this book on the shelf and make it a one-and-done. That won't keep the inner critic at bay. Authentic You and the work you've put in here deserve better anyway.

Keep this book out where you can easily reach for it and return to the sections that resonated most or were the most difficult. Revisit the Pause & Practice section. These exercises can be revisited to boost your confidence in how far you've come and to refuel you when you're feeling weary and defeated. We all have those days.

And finally, be so proud of yourself, my fine, courageous friend.

You're doing it! Keep climbing.

And never forget…

I'm always cheering you on!

Review Inquiry

Hey, it's me!

I hope you've enjoyed the book, finding it both useful and fun. I have a humble request.

Would you consider giving it a rating wherever you bought the book? Online book stores are more likely to promote a book when they feel good about its content, and reader reviews are a great barometer for a book's quality.

So please go to the website of wherever you bought the book, search for my name and the book title, and leave a review. If able, perhaps consider adding a picture of you holding the book. That increases the likelihood your review will be accepted!

Many thanks in advance! I appreciate you!

MaryAnn

Will You Share the Love?

Get this book for a friend, associate, or family member!

If you have found this book valuable and know others who would find it useful, consider buying them a copy as a gift. Special bulk discounts are available if you would like your whole teamor organization to benefit from reading it. Just contact hello@calmyourinnercritic.com or go to https://www.calmyourinnercritic.com.

Would You Like MaryAnn Gramig to Speak to Your Organization?

Book MaryAnn Now!

MaryAnn is an in-demand keynote speaker. To learn how you can bring her message to your organization, email hello@calmyourinnercritic.com or visit https://www.calmyourinnercritic.com.

Would You Like to Engage MaryAnn Gramig as a Coach?

MaryAnn accepts a limited number of coaching clients each year. To learn how to engage her, email hello@calmyourinnercritic.com or visit https://www.calmyourinnercritic.com.

Resources for Further Growth

What's Your Inner Critic's Personality Quiz

Enjoy reflecting on your relationship with your inner critic as you take this FREE 2-minute quiz. Afterward, you'll receive immediate results and messages from MaryAnn with more insights and practical guidance to help you calm your type of inner critic.

Take the free quiz https://www.calmyourinnercritic.com/whats-your-inner-critics-personality

Calm Your Inner Critic Video Course

Want more guidance as you navigate the material in this book? In the video course, MaryAnn breaks down all the concepts you learned in this book, spread across 6 weeks, so you can absorb each idea, apply what makes sense to your life, and keep adding new tools and techniques to cultivate Authentic You.

Learn more about the Course here:
https://www.calmyourinnercritic.com/course

Acknowledgments

Without Jack Charles, you would not be holding this book in your hands. Because of his vision and encouragement, his spouse and my amazing editor, Dr. Cindy Childress, chose to be the expert literary editor, businesswoman, and fairy godmother to budding authors like me from all over the world. Without her, I couldn't have written one word worth reading. Cindy, you're incredible at what you do—helping to get the words in both our hearts and minds onto the page.

To Everett O'Keefe, Malia Sexton, and Zelda Fogle at Ignite Press, your enthusiasm for my book is humbling. Thank you for wanting it to bear your trademark.

To JP Gramig, Kyle and Katie Gramig, David Cook, Carla Nye, Cheryl Van Stockum, Sandy Evenson, Charnel Burton, Sara Harvey, Stacy Rogers, Katie Fussenegger, Shanna Hernandez, Noel Lambert Riley, Dinah McLemore, Shannon Darst, Jeff Crowe, Kahlil and Kristi Flesher, Dianne Gramig, thank you for your support of the work of this book and for being an integral part of it coming to life.

Thank you to Logan Flesher, my nephew, and *Old Yeller* fan, who kept asking. You encouraged me during the early phase when, at times, writing this book felt too hard.

For everyone who helped spread the word about *The Howl of the Whisper,* ushering it into the public eye and buying copies for friends and family, I could not have launched this project without you. Thank you from the bottom of my heart.

To my past and current clients, it's an honor to know you and watch you step up to that which is difficult with perseverance, unique style, and grit. To every organization that trusts me with your most valuable assets—your people—I am humbled.

To my amazing team at AuthenticA: three strong, brilliant, independent businesswomen who keep me straight every day, Angela Kizska, Kim Hazelton, and Ellen Elmore. I greatly appreciate your intellect, expertise, and commitment to keep AuthenticA running while I was off in a cabin somewhere in the woods writing.

And finally, and importantly, to my spouse, Keith, who said "I do" 39 years ago. Thank you for standing by me.

About the Author

MaryAnn Gramig always found herself in the role of "leader," since her early days bossing all the other kids around at summer camp. She eventually channeled that energy into positive expressions as a C-suite non-profit executive. Motivated by her own childhood trauma, she dedicated nine years working in the anti-obscenity/sex trafficking field. Regarded as The Leader's Life Coach, she brings fearless insights to problem solving and always helps her clients execute to the goal.

She is the founder and CEO of AuthenticA, a coaching and consulting firm and holds degrees from the University of Louisville and Florida International University. She is a recipient of the Department of Defense National Meritorious Public Service Award, the third-highest honor a civilian can receive.

She has lived in South Korea, Hawaii, and seven other U.S. states. MaryAnn loves driving supercars, and you will often find her on stage as part of an award-winning regional acting company performing Shakespeare and contemporary plays. She is married with three children, five grandchildren, and lives in the heart of Kentucky's bourbon and horse country. Her beagle, Daisy, and cat, Norman, would like to say they love the book and seeing their names on the back cover.

MaryAnn can be reached at: https://www.calmyourinnercritic.com

www.ingramcontent.com/pod-product-compliance
Lightning Source LLC
Chambersburg PA
CBHW060435130626
46555CB00005B/2369